10568571

lebor ʒabala erenn

Translated by: R.A.S. Macalister
Edited and illustrated by: D.P. Curtin

Dalcassian
Publishing
Company

PHILADELPHIA, PA

Library of Congress Cataloging-in-Publication Data
Copyright © 2018 Dalcassian Publishing Co.
In association with St. Macartan Press
All rights reserved.

book i

+ **1**. In principio fecit Deus Cawlum et Terram, i.e., God made Heaven and Earth at the first, [and He Himself hath no beginning nor ending].

+ **2**. He made first the formless mass, and the light of angels, [on the first Sunday]. He made firmament [on the Monday]. He made earth and seas [on the Tuesday]. He made sun and moon and the stars of Heaven [on the Wednesday]. He made birds [of the air] and reptiles [of the sea on the Thursday]. He made beasts [of the earth] in general, and Adam to rule over them, [on the Friday]. Thereafter God rested [on the Saturday] from the accomplishment of a new Creation, [but by no means from its governance].

+ **3**. [Thereafter] He gave the bailiffry of Heaven to Lucifer, with the nine orders of the Angels of Heaven. He gave the bailiffry of Earth to Adam [and to Eve, with her progeny]. [Thereafter] Lucifer sinned, so that he was leader of a third of the host of angels. The King confined him with a third of the host of angels in his company, in Hell. And God said unto the Foe of Heaven: [Haughty is this Lucifer], unite et confundamus consilium eius.

+ 4. Thereafter Lucifer had envy against Adam, for he was assured that this would be given him [Adam], the filling of Heaven in his [Lucifer's] room. Wherefore he [Iofer Niger] came in the form of the serpent, and persuaded [Adam and] Eve to sin, in the matter of eating of the apple from the forbidden tree. Wherefore Adam was expelled from Paradise into common earth.

+ **5**. Thereafter the Lord came to them, and He said unto Adam, Terra es et in terram ibis [i.e., of earth was he made and into earth shall he go]. In sudore uultus fui comedes panem tuum [i.e., he shall not obtain satisfaction without labor]. He said further unto the woman: Cum dolore et gemitu paries filios tuos et filias tuas [i.e., it shall be with ... insufferable pain that thou shalt bring forth thy sons].

+ **6**. The progeny of Adam sinned [thereafter], namely the elder of the sons of Adam, Cain the accursed, who slew his brother Abel ... [through his jealousy?] and through his greed, with the bone of a camel, as learned men say. [In this manner] began the kin-murders of the world.

+ **7**. As for Seth, one of the three sons of Adam [who had progeny], of him are the men of the whole world. Noe son of Lamech son of Mathusalem son of Enoch son of Iared son of Malalahel son of Cainan son of Enos son of Seth son of Adam, For it is Noe who is the second Adam, to whom the men of all the world are traced. For the Flood drowned the whole seed of Adam, except Noe with his three sons, Sem, Ham, Iafeth, and their four wives Coba, Olla, Oliva, Olivana. Afterwards, when God brought a Flood over the whole world, none of the people of the world escaped from the Flood except it be the people of that ark - Noe with his three sons, and the wife of Noe, the wives of his sons.

Ut dixit poeta,
A host that a wintry death would not subdue
Noe, there was no hero's weakness,
A story with horror has been made clear with keenness
Sem, Ham, and Iafeth.

Women without evil colour, great excellences,
above the Flood without extinctions,
Coba, vigorous was the white swan,
Olla, Oliva, Olivana.

+ **8**. Now Sem settled in Asia, Ham in Africa, Iafeth in Europe -

Sem settled in pleasant Asia;
Ham with his progeny in Africa noble Iafeth and his
sons, it is they who settled in Europe.

Sem had thirty sons, including Arfaxad, Assur, and Persius. Ham had thirty sons, including Chus and Chanaan. Iafeth had fifteen including Dannai, Gregus, Hispanius, Gomer. Or it is twenty-seven sons that Sem had.

Thirty sleek sons, a brilliant fact,
they sprang from Ham, son of Noe
twenty-seven who are from Sem,
and fifteen from Iafeth.

+ **9**. [With regard to] Iafeth [son of Noe], of him is the northern side of Asia - namely Asia Minor, Armenia, Media, the People of Scythia; and of him are the inhabitants of all Europe. Grecus son of Iafeth, of him is Grecia Magna, Grecia Parva and Alexandian Greece. Espanus son of Iafeth from whom are the Hispani. Gomer son of Iafeth had two sons, Emoth and

6

Ibath. Emoth, of him is the northern people of the world. Ibath had two sons, Bodb and Baath. Bodb, who had a son Dohe.

Elinus son of Dohe had three sons, Airmen, Negua, Isacon. As for Airmen, he had five sons, Gutus, Cebidus, Uiligothus, Burgundus, Longbardus. Negua had three sons, Saxus, Boarus, Uandalus. Isacon, moreover, one of the three sons of Elenus, he had four sons, Romanus, Francus, Britus, Albanus. This is that Albanus who first took Albania, with his children, and of him is Alba named: so he drove his brother across the Sea of Icht, and from him are the Albanians of Latium of Italy.

+ **10**. Magog, son of Iafeth, of his progeny are the peoples who came to Ireland before the Gaedil: to wit Partholan son of Sera son of Sru son of Esru son of Bimbend (sic) son of Magog son of Iafeth; and Nemed son of Agnomain son of Pamp son of Tat son of Sera son of Sru; and the progeny of Nemed, the Gaileoin, Fir Domnann, Fir Bolg and Tuatha De Danann. As the poet said,

> *Magog son of Iafeth there is*
> *cerainty of his progeny;*
> *of them was Parthalon of Banba*
> *--decorous was his achievement.*

Of them was noble Nemed son of Agnomain, unique; of them were Gand and Genand, Sengand, free Slaine. The numerous progeny of Elada, of them was Bres, no untruth: son of Elada expert in arms, son of Delbaeth son of Net. SON OF Inda, son of Allda -Allda who was son of Tat, son of Tabarn son of Enda, son of Baath, [son of] pleasant Ibath. son of Bethach son of Iardan son of Nemed grandson of Paimp: Pamp son of Tat son of Sera son of Sru son of white Braiment. Of Braiment son of Aithecht, son of Magog, great in reknown: there happened in their time a joint appearance against a Plain.

+ **11**. Baath, [one of the two sons of Ibath] son of Gomer son of Iafeth, of him are the Gaedil and the people of Scythia. He had a son, the noble eminent man whose name was Feinus Farsaid. [It is he who was one of the seventy-two chieftains who went for the building of Nemrod's Tower, whence the languages were dispersed.] Howbeit, Nemrod himself was son of Cush son of Ham son of Noe. This is that Feinius aforesaid who brought the People's Speech from the Tower: and it is he who had the great school, learning the multiplicity of languages.

7

+ **12**. Now Feinius had two sons: Nenual, [one of the two] whom he left in the princedom of Scythia behind him; Nel, the other son, at the Tower was he born. Now he was a master of all the languages; wherefore one came [to summon him] from pharao, in order to learn the multiplicity of languages from him. But Feinius came out of Asia to Scythia, whence he had gone for the building of the Tower; so that he died in the princedom of Scythia, at the end of forty years, and passed on the chieftainship to his son, Nenual.

+ **13**. At the end of forty-two years after the building of the Tower, Ninus son of Belus took the kingship of the world. For no other attempted to exercise authority over the peoples or to bring the multitude of nations under one had, and under tax and tribute, but he alone. Aforetime there had been chieftains; he who was noblest and most in favour in the community, he it was who was chief counsellor for every man: who should avert all injustice and further all justice. No attempt was made to invade or to dominate other nations.

+ **14**. Now that is the time when Gaedel Glas, [from whom are the Gaedil] was born, of Scota daughter of the Pharao. From her are the Scots named, ut dictum est:

> *Feni are named from Feinius*
> *a meaning without secretiveness:*
> *Gaedil from comely Gaedel Glas,*
> *Scots from Scota.*

+ **15**. It is Gaedel Glas who fashioned the Gaelic language out of the seventy-two languages: there are their names, Bithynian, Scythian, etc. Unde poeta cecinit:

> *The languages of the world, see for yourselves*
> *Bithynia, Scythia, Cilicia, Hyreania,*
> *Gothia, Graecia, Germania, Gallia with horror,*
> *Pentapolis, Phrygia, Palmatia, Dardania.*
>
> *Pamphylia, Mauretania, populous Lycaonia,*
> *Bacctria, Creta, Corsica,*
> *Cypros Thessalia, Cappadocia, noble Armenia,*
> *Raetia, Sicilia, Saracen-land, Sardinia.*
>
> *Belgia, Boeotia, Brittania, tuneful Rhodos,*

8

Hispania, Roma, Rhegini, Phoenicia,
India, golden Arabia,
Mygdonia, Mazaca, Macedonia.

Parthia, Caria, Syria, Saxones,
Athenae, Achaia, Albania,
Hebraei Arcadia, clear Galatia,
Troas. Thessalia, Cyclades.

Moesia, Media, Persida, Franci,
Cyrene, Lacedaemonia, Langobardi,
Thracia, Numidia, Hellas (?)
-- hear it! Lofty Italia, Ethipia, Egypt.

That is the tally of languages
without tarnish out of which Gaedel cut Gaedelic:
known to me is their roll of understanding,
the groups, the manifold languages.

+ **16**. Now Sru son of Esru son of Gaedel, he it is who was chieftain for the Gaedil who went out of Egypt after Pharao was drowned [with his host in the Red Sea of Israel]: Seven hundred and seventy years from the Flood till then. Four hundred and forty years from that time in which Pharao was drowned, and after Sru son of Esru came out of Egypt, till the time when the sons of Mil came into Ireland, to wit, Eber and Eremon: hereanent [one] said--

Forty and four hundred of years--it is no falsehood--
from when the people of God came,
be ye certain over the surface of Mare Rubrum,
till they landed in Scene from the clear sea,
they, the Sons of Mil, in the land of Ireland.

+ **17**. Four ships' companies strong went Sru out of Egypt. There were twenty-four wedded couples and three hirelings for every ship. Sru and his son Eber Scot, they were the chieftains of the expedition. [It is then that Nenual son of Baath son of Nenual son of Feinius Farsaid, prince of Scythia, died: and] Sru also died immediately after reaching Scythia.

+ **18**. Eber Scot took [by force] the kingship of Scythia from the progeny of Nenual, till he fell at the hands of Noemius son of Nenual. There was a contention between Noemius and Boamain son of Eber Scot. Boamain

9

took the kingship till he fell at the hands of Noemius. Noemius took the princedom till he fell at the hands of Ogamain son of Boamain in vengeance for this father. Ogamain took the kingship till he died. Refill son of Noemius took the kingship till he fell at the hands of Tat son of Ogamain. Thereafter Tat fell at the hands of Refloir son of Refill. Thereafter there was a contention for the princedom between Refloir [grandson of Noemius and Agnomain son of Tat, until Refloir fell at the hands of Agnomain.

+ **19**. For that reason was the seed of Gaedil driven forth upon the sea, to wit Agnomain and Lamfhind his son, so that they were seven years on the sea, skirting the world on the north side. More than can be reckoned are the hardships which they suffered. [The reason why the name Lamfhind was given to the son of Agnomain was, because not greater was the radiance of candles than his hands, at the towing.] They had three ships with a coupling between them, that none of them should move away from the rest. They had three chieftains after the death of Agnomain on the surface of the great Caspian Sea, Lamfhind and Allot and Caicher the druid.

+ **20**. It is Caicher the druid who gave the remedy to them, when the Siren was making melody to them: sleep was overcoming them at the music. This is the remedy which Caicher found for them, to melt wax in their ears. It is Caicher who spoke to them, when the great wind drove them into the Ocean, so that they suffered much with hunger and thirst there: till at the end of a week they reached the great promontory which is northward from the Rhipaean Mountain, and in that promontory they found a spring with the taste of wine, and they feasted there, and were three days and three nights asleep there. But Caicher the druid said: Rise, said he, we shalal not rest until we reach Ireland. What place is that 'Ireland' said Lamfhind son of Agnomain. Further than Scythia is it, said Caicher. It is not ourselves who shall reach it, but our children, at the end of three hundred years from today.

+ **21**. Thereafter they settled in the Macotic Marshes, and there a son was born to Lamfhind, Eber Glunfhind: [white marks which were on his knees]. He it is who was chieftain after his father.
His grandson was Febri [Glunfhind (Sic)]. His grandson was Nuadu.

+ **22**. Brath son of Death son of Ercha son of Allot son of Nuadu son of Nenual son of Febri Glas son of Agni find son of Eber Glunfhind son of Lamfhind son of Agnomain son of Tat son of Agnomain son of Boamain son of Eber Scot son of Sru son of Esru son of Gaedel Glas son of Nel son of Feinius Farsaid: It is that Brath who came out of the Marshes along the Torrian Sea to Crete and to Sicily. They reached spain thereafter. They took Spain by force.

+ **23**. As for Agnomain son of Tat, he is the leader of the Gaedil who came out of Scythia. He had two sons, Lamfhind and Allot. Lamfhind had one son, Eber Glunfhind. Allot had a son, Eber Dub, at the same time as the sojourn in the Marshes. They had two grandsons in joint rule, Toithecht son of Tetrech son of Eber Dub, and Nenual son of Febri son of Agni son of Eber Glunfhind; there was also Soithecht son of Mantan son of Caicher. Ucce and Occe, two sons of Allot son of Nenual son of Nemed son of Allot son of Ogamain son of Toithecht son of Tetrech son of Eber Dub son of Allot.

+ **24**. Four ships' companies strong came the Gaedil to Spain: in every ship fourteen wedded couples and seven unwed hirelings. Brath, a ship's company. Ucce and Occe, two ships' companies: [Two brethren were they, the sons of Allot son of Nenual son of Nemed son of Allot son of Ogamain], Mantan [son of Caicher the druid son of Ercha son of

11

(Coemthecht)] a ship's company. So they broke three battles after going into Spain: a battle against the Tuscans, a battle against the Langobardi, and a battle against the Barchu. But there came a plague upon them, and four and twenty of their number died, including Occe and Ucce. Out of the two ships none escaped, save twice five men, including En son of Occe and Un sons of Ucce.

+ **25**. Brath had a good son named Breogan, by whom was built the Tower and the city - Braganza was the city's name. From Breogan's Tower it was that Ireland was seen; an evening of a day of winter Ith son of Breogan saw it. Unde Gilla Coemain cecinit--

> *Gaedel Glas, of whom are the Gaedil,*
> *son was he of Nel, with store of wealth:*
> *he was mighty west and east,*
> *Nel, son of Feinius Farsaid.*
>
> *Feinius had two sons--I speak truth--*
> *Nel our father and Nenual,*
> *Nel was born at the Tower in the east,*
> *Nenual in Scythia, bright as a shield.*
>
> *After Feinius, the hero of ocean,*
> *there was great envy between the brethren:*
> *Nel slew Nenual, who was not gentle;*
> *the High King was expelled.*
>
> *He went into Egypt through valour*
> *till he reached powerful Pharao;*
> *till he bestowed Scota, of no scanty beauty,*
> *the modest, nimble daughter of pharao.*
>
> *Scota bore a son to noble Nel,*
> *from whom was born a perfect great race:*
> *Gaedel Glas was the name of the man--*
> *green were his arms and his vesture.*
>
> *Fierce Esru was son to him,*
> *who was a Lord with heavy arms:*
> *the son of Esru, Sru of the ancient hosts*
> *to whom was meet all the fame attributed to him.*

Sru son of Esru son of Gaedel,
our ancestor, rejoicing in troops,
he it is who went northward to his house,
over the surface of the red Mare Rubrum.

The crews of four ships were the tale
of his host along the red Mare Rubrum:
in his house of planks, we may say,
twenty-four wedded couples.

The prince of Scythia, it ws a clear fact,
the youth whose name was Nenual,
it is then he died yonder in his house--
when the Gaedil arrived.

Eber Scot of the heroes assumed [the kingdom]
over the progeny of Nenual unashamed,
till he fell, with no gentle kindness,
at the hands of Noemius son of Nenual.

The strong son of Eber thereafter, who had the name Boamain,
of perfect purity, to the shore
of the Caspian Sea was he king,
till he fell by the hand of Noemius.

Noemius son of Nenual of the strength
settled in Scythia, chequered like a shield:
the perfect fair prince fell
by the hand of Ogamain son of Boamain.

Thereafter Ogamain was prince
after Noemius of good strength:
till he died in his territory, unchurched:
after him Refill was king.

Thereafter Refill fell by
the hand of Tait son of Ogmain:
Tait fell, though he was not feeble,'
by the hand of Refloir son to Refill.

Refloir and Agnomain without blemish,
seven years were they in contention,

13

till Refloir fell with tumult
by the victorious hand of Agnomain.

Noinel and Refill with a [spear] point
two sons of Refloir son of Refill,
they drove Agnomain out over the raging sea,
great and green.

Good were the chieftains, it was sufficient,
who came out of Scythia;
Agnomain, Eber without blemish,
the two sons of Tait son of Ogamain.

Allot, Lamfhind of the green hand,
conspicuous the two sons of very bright Agnomain,
Caicher and Cing, fame with victory
the two good sons of Eber of the red-steed.

The number of their ships,
three ships coming over heavy waves;
three score [the crew] of every ship,
a clear saying, and women every third score.

Agnomain died, it was no reproach
in the islands of the great Caspian Sea.
The place where they were for a year
they found very secret.

They reached the full Libyan Sea,
a sailing of six complete summer days;
Glas son of Agnomain, who was not dspicable,
died there in Cercina.

A fair island found they there
on the Libyan Sea of warrior-blades:
a season over a year, with fame,
their sojourn in that island.

They sail on the sea,
a brilliant fact both by day and by night:
the sheen of the hands of lustrous Lamfhind
was like to fair candles.

14

Four chieftains had they who were not despicable,
after coming over the Libyan Sea:
Allot, Lamfhind wsift over the ocean,
Cing and his brother Caicher.

Caicher found a remedy for them
yonder for the melody of the Sirens:
this is the remedy that fair Caicher found,
to melt wax in their ears.

They found a spring and a land
at the Rhipaean headland with great might,
having the taste of wine thereafter:
their thirst overcame them mightily.

Soundly, soundly they slept
to the end of three days without sorrow,
till Caicher the faithful druid wakened
the noble men impatiently.

It is Caicher, (a brilliant fulfilment!)
who made a prophecy to them,
at the Rhipaean Mountains with a headland--
"We have no rest until Ireland."

"In what place is lofty Ireland?"
said Lamfhind the violent warrior.
"Very far" said Caicher then,
"It is not we who reach it, but our children."

They advanced in their battalion with venom,
southward past the Rhipaean headlands;
the progeny of Gaedel, with purity,
they landed at the Marshes.

A glorious son was born there
to Lamfhind son of Agnomain;
Eber Glunfhind, pure the gryphon,
the curl-haired grandfather of Febri.

The family of Gaedel, the brisk and white,

15

were three hundred years in that land:
they dwelt there thenceforward,
until Brath the victorious came.

Brath, the noble son of Faithful Death
came to Crete, to Sicily,
the crew of four ships of a safe sailing,
right-hand to Europe, on to Spain.

Occe and Ucce without blemish,
the two sons of Allot son of Nenual;
Mantan son of Caicher, faithful Brath,
they were the four leaders.

Fourteen men with their wives
made the crew for every ship full of warriors,
and six noble hirelings;
they won three battles in Spain.

Lofty the first battle - I shall not conceal it
--which they won against the host of the Tuscans;
a battle against the Bachra with violence,
and a battle against the Langobardi.

It was after the sinister battle
that there came to them a plague of one day:
the people of the ships of the sons of Allot
without fault were all dead except ten persons.

Un and En came out of it,
two noble sons of the strong chieftains:
thereafter was Bregon born,
father of Bile the strong and raging.

He broke a great number of fights and battles
against the many-coloured host of Spain:
Bregon of the shouts of valorous deeds,
of the combats, by him was built Brigantia.

Bregon son of Brath, gentle and good,
he had a son, Mil:
the seven sons of Mil--good their host--

16

including Eber and Eremon.

Along with Dond, and Airech with battle,
including Ir, along with Arannan,
including Armorgen with bright countenance,
and along with Colptha of the sword.

The ten sons of Bregon without falsehood,
Brega, Fuat, and Murthemne,
Cualnge, Cuala, fame though it were,
Ebleo, Nar, Ith, and Bile.

Ith son of Bregon with tuneful fame
came at the first into Ireland:
he is the first of men who inhabited it,
of the noble seed of the powerful Gaedil.

book ii

+ **26**. Let us cease [at this point] from the stories of the Gaedil, that we may tell of the seven peoples who took Ireland before them. Cessair, daughter of Bith son of Noe took it, forty days before the Flood. Partholon son of Sera three hundred years after the Flood. Nemed son of Agnomain of the Greeks of Scythia, at the end of thirty years after Partholon. The Fir Bolg thereafter. The Fir Domnann thereafter. The Gailioin thereafter [al., along with them]. The Tuatha De Danann thereafter. [The sons of Mil thereafter as Fintan said]. Unde Fintan cecinit:

Ireland--whatever is asked of me
I know pleasantly,
Every taking that took her
from the beginning of the tuneful world.

Cessair came from the East,
the woman was daughter of Bith;
with her fifty maidens,
with her three men.

Flood overtook Bith in his Mountain,
it is no secret;
Ladra in Ard Ladrand,
Cessair in her Nook.

But as for me, He buried me,
the Son of God, above [the] company;
He snatched the Flood from me
above heavy Tul Tuinde.

I had a year under the Flood
in strong Tul Tuinde;
I found nothing for my sustenance,
an unbroken sleep were best.

I was in Ireland here,
my journey was everlasting,
till Partholon reached her,

18

from the East, from the land of Greeks.

I was here in Ireland
and Ireland was desert,
till the son of Agnomain reached Nemed,
brilliant his fashion.

The Fir Bolg and Fir Gailian came,
it was long ago;
the Fir Domnann came,
they landed on a headland in the west.

Thereafter the Tuath De came,
in their masses of fog,
so that there was sustenance for me
though it was a long lifetime.

The sons of Mil came from Spain,
from the south, so that there
was sustenance for me at their hands,
though they were strong in battle.

A long life fell to my lot,
I shall not conceal it;
till Faith overtook me
from the King of Heaven of clouds.

I am Fintan the white son of Bochna,
I shall not conceal it;
after the Flood here I am
a noble great sage.

+ **27**. Incipit de The Takings of Ireland. Thereafter Cessair daughter of Bith son of Noe took it, ut poeta dixit, forty days before the Flood. This is the reason for her coming, fleeing from the Flood: for Noe said unto them: Rise, said he [and go] to the western edge of the world; perchance the Flood may not reach it.

+ **28**. The crew of three ships arrived at Dun na mRarc in the territory of Corco Daibne. Two of the ships were wrecked. Cessair with the crew of her ship escaped, fifty women and three men: Bith son of Noe, of whom is

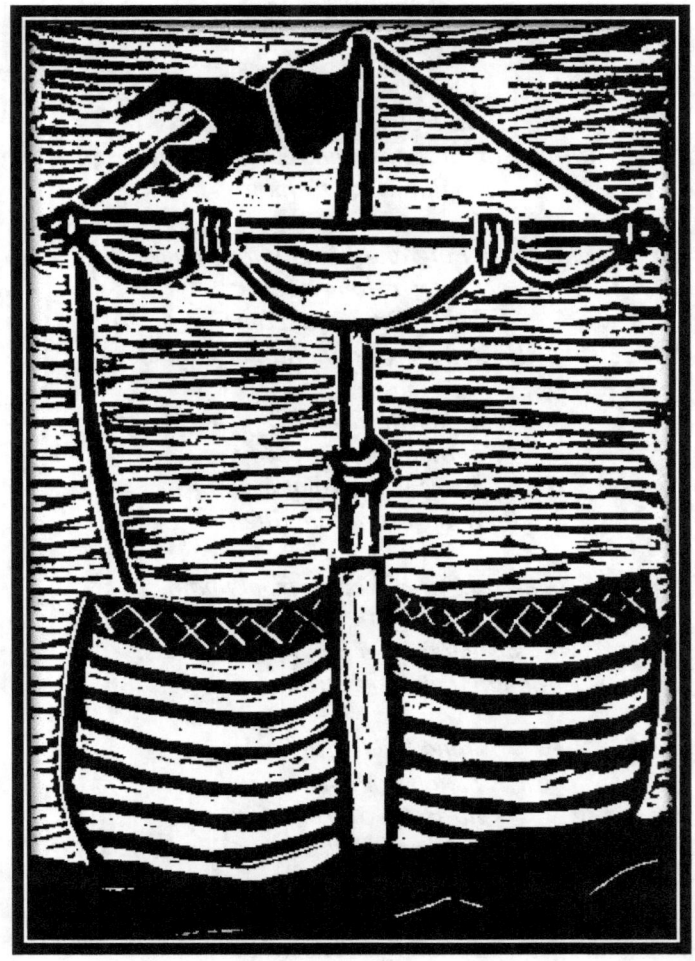

Sliab Betha (named) - there was he buried, in the great stone-heap of Sliab Betha; Ladra the pilot, of whom is Ard Ladrand - he is the first dead man who went under the soil of Ireland; Fintan son of Bochra, of whom is "Fintan's Grave" over Tul Tuinde. Cessair died in Cul Cessrach in Connachta, with her fifty maidens.

+ **29**. These are their names, ut Fintan cecinit:

> *A just division we shared between us,*
> *myself and Bith and bold Ladra;*
> *for peace and for reason was it done,*

in the matter of the fifty magnificent maidens.

Seventeen women I took, including Cessair--
Lot, Luam, Mall, Mar, Froechar, Femar, Faible, Foroll,
Cipir, Torrian, Tamall, Tam, Abba, Alla, Baichne, Sille:
that is the tale which we were there.

Seventeen Bith took, with Bairrfhind--
Sella, Della, Duib, Addeos, Fotra, Traige, Nera, Buana,
Tamall, Tanna, Nathra, Leos, Fodarg, Rodarg, Dos, Clos:
be it heard -those were our people further.

Sixteen thereafter with Ladra:
Alba, Bona, Albor, Ail, Gothiam, German, Aithne,
Inde, Rodarg, Rinne, Inchor, Ain, Irrand, Espa, Sine, Samoll:
that was our fair company.

None of the seed of Adam took Ireland before the Flood but those.

+ **30**. Now Ireland was waste [thereafter], for a space of three hundred years, [or three hundred and twelve, quod uerius est] till Partholon son of Sera son of Sru came to it. He is the first who took Ireland after the Flood, on a Tuesday, on the fourteenth of the moon, in Inber Scene: [for three times was Ireland taken in Inber Scene]. Of the progeny of Magog son of Iafeth was he, [ut dixi supra]: in the sixstieth year of the age of Abraham, Partholon took Ireland.

+ **31**. Four chieftains strong came Partholon: himself and Laiglinne his son, from whom is Loch Laighlinne in Ui mac Uais of Breg; Slanga and Rudraige, the two other sons of Partholon, from whom are Sliab Slanga and Loch Rudraige. When the grave of Rudraige was a-digging, the lake there burst forth over the land.

+ **32**. Seven years had Partholon in Ireland when the first man of his people died, to wit, Fea, from whom is Mag Fea; for there was he buried, in Mag Fea.

+ **33**. In the third year thereafter, the first battle of Ireland, which Partholon won in Slemna of Mag Itha against Cichol clapperlag of the Fomoraig. Men with single arms and single legs they were, who joined the battle with him.

+ **34**. There were seven lake bursts in Ireland in the time of Partholon:
Loch Laighlinne in Ui mac Uais of Breg, Loch Cuan and Loch Rudraige in
Ulaid, Loch Dechet and Loch Mese and Loch Con in Connachta, and Loch
Echtra in Airgialla; for Partholon did not find more than three lakes and
nine rivers in Ireland before him--Loch Fordremain in Sliab Mis of Mumu,
Loch Lumnig on Tir Find, Loch Cera in Irrus; Aba Life, Lui, Muad,
Slicech, Samer (upon which is Ess Ruaid), Find, Modorn, Buas, and Banna
between Le and Elle. Four years before the death of Partholon, the burst of
Brena over the land.

+ **35**. Four plains were cleared by Partholon in Ireland: Mag Itha in Laigen,
Mag Tuired in Connachta, Mag Li in Ui mac Uais, Mag Ladrand in Dal
nAraide. For Partholon found not more than one plain in Ireland before
him, the Old Plain [of Elta] of Edar. this is why it is called the "Old Plain"
for never did branch of twig of a wood grow through it.

+ **36**. And it is there that Partholon died, five thousand men and four
thousand women, of a week's plague on the kalends of May. On a Monday
plauge killed them all except one man tantum--Tuan son of Starn son of
Sera nephew of Partholon: and God fashioned him in many forms, and that
man survived alone from the time of Partholon to the time of Findian and
of Colum Cille. So he narrated to them the Takings of Ireland from the
time of Cessair, the first who took, to that time. And that is Tuan son of
Cairell son of Muiredach Muinderg. Of him the history-sage sang the
following song—

Ye scholars of the Plain of fair, white Conn,
of the land of the men of Fal, as I relate,
what company, after the creation of the world,
first lighted upon Ireland?

Ireland before the swift Flod,
as I reckon her courses, knowing,
pure-white kemps found her,
including Cessair daughter of Bith.

Bith son of Noe of the many troops,
though he overcame with a trench-achievement,
he died in warlike Sliab Betha;
Ladra died in Ard Ladrann.

Fintain went on a journey of weakness,

22

his grave was found, it ws a leap of impetuosity;
he was not in haste into the trench of a churchyeard,
but a grave over Tul Tuinde.

To Dun na mBarc for a separation-festival
faring without scale of reckoning brought them;
at the stone-heap, beside a fruitful sea
Cessair died in Cul Cessrach.

Forty days full-scanty the slender and
graceful troop arrived in their ship,
before the noise of the Flood they landed
on a place of the land of Ireland.

He rose on a journey for truth-deciding by the might
of the King whom he used to adore;
Fintan, who was a man with tidings for lords,
for mighty ones of the earth.

Three hundred years, I boast of it,
I speak through the rules which I reckon,
pleasant Ireland, I proclaim it against
the soothsayers was waste, after the Flood.

Partholon the eminent came,
a royal course across an oar-beaten sea:
his quartet of heroes, fair and faithful--
among them was the free-born Slanga.

Slanga, Laiglinne the brilliant,
boardlike, noble and strong was his canoe;
these were his ready trio of chieftains,
along with the lordly Rudraige.

Plains were cleared of their great wood,
by him, to get near to his dear children;
Mag Itha southward, a hill of victory-head,
Mag Li of ashes, Lag Lathraind.

Seven lake-bursts, though ye measure them,
with renown of name,
though ye should set them forth they filled,

23

amid the fetter of valleys, insular Ireland in his time.

Loch Laiglinne, bold Loch Cuan,
the Loch of Rudraige, (he was) a lord without law-giving,
Loch Techet, Loch Oese abounding in mead,
Loch Cou, Loch Echtra full of swans.

Over Ireland of beauty of colour,
as I relate every foundation
on the fortress of Bith
he found not more than three lakes before him.

Three lakes, vast and tideless (?)
and nine rivers full of beauty:
Loch Fordremain, Loch Luimnig,
Findloch over the borders of Irrus.

The river of Life, the Lee let us mention,
which every druid humms who knows diana senga;
the history of the old rivers of Ireland
has demonstrated the true height of the Flood.

Muad, Slicech, Samer, thou dost name it, Buas,
a flood with the fame-likeness of a summit, Modorn,
Find with fashion of a sword-blade (?)
Banna between Lee and Eille.

He died after pride, with warriors,
Partholon, of the hundredfold troop:
they were cut down with possessions,
with treasures, on the Old Plain of Elta of Edar.

This is why it is the forutnate Old Plain
It is God the fashioner who caused it:
over its land which the sea-mouth cut off
no root or twig of a wood was found.

His grave is there according to men of truth,
Although he had no power among saints:
Silent was his sleep under resting places
which are no pilgrimage-way for our scholars.

Three hundred years, though ye should know it,
over lands secret to the exalted,
had the troop, brightly tuneful and lasting,
over age-old, noble Ireland.

Men, women, boys and girls,
on the calends of May, a great hindrance,
the plaguing of Partholon in Mag Breg
was no unbroken summer-apportionment of peace.

It was thirty lean years that she
was empty in the face of war-champions,
after the death of her host throughout a week,
in their troops upon Mag Elta.

Let us give adoration to the King of the Elements,
to the good Head, the Fortress of our people,
whose is every troop, every generation,
whose is every head, every scholarship.

I am Ua Flaind who scatters truths;
an apportionment with kings hath he chosen;
may everything whatsoever he may say be a speech of grace,
may it accord with holiness, ye scholars!

+ **37**. It was the four sons of Partholon who made the first division of Ireland in the beginning, Er, Orba, Fergna, Feron. There were four men, namesakes to them, amoung the sons of Mil, but they were not the same. From Ath Cliath of Laigen to Ailech Neit, is the division of Er. From Ath Cliath to the island of Ard Nemid, is the division of Orba. From Ailech to Ath Cliath of Medraige, is the division of Feron. From that Ath Cliath to Ailech Neit, is the division of Fergna. So that is that manner they first divided Ireland.

+ **38**. Partholon had four oxen, that is the first cattle of Ireland. Of his company was Brea, son of Senboth, by whom were a jouse, a flesh [cauldron], and dwelling first made in Ireland. Of his company was Samailiath, by whom were ale-drinking and suretyship first made in Ireland. Of his company was Beoir, by whom a guesthouse was first made in Ireland. As the poet saith:

Partholon, whence he came to Ireland,
reckon ye!
on the day when he reached across the sea,
what was the land from which Partholon came?

He came from Sicily to Greece--
a year's journey, with no full falsehood:
a month's sailing from Greece westward,
to Cappadocia.

From Cappadocia he journeyed,
a sailing of three days to Gothia,
a sailing of a month from white Gothia,
to three-cornered Spain.

After that he reached Inis Fail,
to Ireland from Spain:
on Monday, the tenth without blemish
one octad took Ireland.

He is the first man who took his wife
in the time of Partholon without falsehood:
Fintan, who took the woman through combat--
Aife, daughter of Partholon.

Parthlolon went out one day,
to tour his profitable land:
His wife and his henchman together
he leaves behind him on the island.

As they were in his house,
the two, a wonder unheard-of,
she made an advance to the pure henchman,
he made no advance to her.

Since he made her no answer promptly the henchman,
stubborn against an evil intention,
she doffs her in desperation--
an impusive action for a good woman!

The henchman rose without uncertainty,
a frail thing is humanity--

and came, a saying without pleasure,
with Deignat to share her couch.

Insolent was the prank for a pleasant henchman
which Topa of tuneful strings wrought:
to go by a rough trick, a happiness without pleasure,
with Delgnat, to share her couch.

Partholon, who was a man of knowledge,
had a vat of most sweet ale:
out of which none could drink aught
save through a tube of red gold.

Thirst seized them after the deed,
Topa and Delgnat, according to truth:
so that their two mouths drank
their two drinks (?) in the tube.

When they did it, a couple without remorse,
there came upon them very great thirst;
soon they drank a bright coal-drink,
through the gilded tube.

Partholon arrived outside,
after ranging the wilderness;
there were given to him,
it was a slight disturbance, his vat and his tube.

When he took the straight tube,
he perceived upon it at once,
the taste of Topa's mouth as far as this,
and the taste of Delgnat's mouth.

A black, curly demon revealed
the bad, false, unpleasant deed:
"Here is the taste of Topa's mouth" said he,
"And the taste of Delgnat's mouth."

Then said the sound son of Sera,
the man called Partholon:
"though short the time we are outside,
we have the right to complain of you."

27

The man smote the woman's dog with his palm
--it was no profit--he slew the hound,
it was a treasure that would be slender;
so that is the first jealousy of Ireland.

Degnat answered her husband:
"Not upon us is the blame,
though bitter thou thinkest my saying it,
truly, but it is upon thee."

Though evil thou thinkest my saying it to thee,
Partholon, its right shall be mine:
I am the 'one before one' here,
I am innocent, recompense is my due.

Honey with a woman, milk with a cat,
food with one generous, meat with a child,
a wright within and an edge[d tool]
one before one, 'tis a great risk.'

The woman will taste the thick honey,
the cat will drink the milk,
the generous will bestow the pure food,
the child will eat the meat.

The wright will lay hold of a tool,
the one with the one will go together:
wherefore it is right to guard them
well from the beginning.

That is the first adultery to be heard of
made here in the beginning:
the wife of Partholon, a man of rank,
to go to an ignoble henchman.

He came after the henchman
and slew him with anger:
to him there came not the help of God
upon the Weir of the Kin-murder.

The place where that was done,

after its fashioning certainty--
great is its sweetness that was there of
a day in the land of Inis Saimera.

And that, without deceit,
is the first judgement in Ireland so that thence,
with very noble judgement,
is "the right of his wife against Partholon."

Seventeen years had they thereafter,
till there came the death of that man;
the battle of Mag Itha of the combats
was one of the deeds of Partholon.

Further of the voyaging of Partholon--

Good was the great company
that Partholon had:
maidens and active youths,
chieftains and champions.

Totacht and strong Tarba,
Eocnar and Aithechbel,
Cuaille, Dorcha, Dam,
the seven chief ploughmen of Partholon.

Liac and Lecmag with colour,
Imar and Etrigi,
the four oxen, a proper group,
who ploughed the land of Partholon.

Beoir was the name of the man,
with his nobles and with his people,
who suffered a guest in his firm house,
the first in Ireland's island.

By that Brea son of Senboth
a house was first, a cauldron on fire;
a feat that the pleasant Gaedil desert not,
dwelling in Ireland.

By Samaliliath were known

ale-drinking and surety-ship:
by him were made thereafter
worship, prayer, questioning.

The three druids of Partholon of the harbours,
Fiss, Eolas, Eochmarc:
the names of his three chamions further,
Milchu, Meran, Muinechan.

The names of the ten noble daughters
whom Partholon had,
and the names of his ten sons-in-law
I have aside, it is a full memory.

Aife, Aine, lofty Adnad,
Macha, Mucha, Melepard,
Glas and Grenach,
Auach and Achanach.

Aidbli, Bomnad and Ban,
Caertin, Echtach, Athchosan,
Lucraid, Ligair, Lughaid the warrior,
Gerber who was not vain of word.

Beothach, Iarbonel, Fergus, Art, Corb,
who followed (?) without sin,
Sobairche, active Dobairche,
were the five chieftains of Nemed, good in strength.

Bacorb Ladra, who was a sound sage,
he was Partholon's man of learning:
he is the first man, without uncertainty,
who made hospitality at the first.

Where they ploughed in the west was at Dun Finntain,
though it was very far:
and they grazed grass of resting
in the east of Mag Sanais.

Bibal and Babal the white,
were Partholon's two merchants:
Bibal brought gold hither,

Babal brought cattle.

The first building of Ireland without sorrow,
was made by Partholon:
the first brewing, churning, ale, a course with grace,
at first, in good and lofty Ireland.

Rimad was the firm tall-ploughman,
Tairle the general head-ploughamn:
Fodbach was the share, no fiction is that,
and Fetain the coulter.

Broken was the name of the man, it was perfect,
who first wrought hidden shamefulness:
it was destroyed with a scattering that was not evil,
Partholon thought this to be good.

So these are the tidings of the first Taking of Ireland after the Flood.

book iii

+ **39**. Now Ireland was waste thereafter, for a space of thirty years after Partholon, till Nemed son of Agnomain of the Greeks of Scythia came thither, with his four chieftains; [they were the four sons of Nemed]. Forty-four ships had he on the Caspian Sea for a year and a half, but his ship alone reached Ireland. These are the four chieftains, Starn, Iarbonel the Soothsayer, Annind, and Fergus Red-Side: they were the four sons of Nemed.

+ **40**. There were four lake-bursts in Ireland in the time of Nemed: Loch Cal in Ui Niallain, Loch Munremair in Luigne, Loch Dairbrech, Loch Annind in Meath. When his grave [of Annind son of Nemed] was being dug and he was a-burying, there the lake burst over the land.

+ **41**. It is Nemed who won the battle of Ros Fraechain against Gand and Sengand, two kings of the Fomoraig, and the twain were slain there. Two royal forts were dug by Nemed in Ireland, Raith Chimbaith in Semne, Raith Chindeich in Ui Niallain. The four sons of Matan Munremar dug Raith Cindeich in one day: namely, Boc, Roboc, Ruibne, and Rotan. They were slain before the morrow in Daire Lige by Nemed, lest they should improve upon the digging.

+ **42**. Twelve plains were cleared by Nemed in Ireland: Mag Cera, Mag Eba, Mag Cuile Tolaid, and Mag Luirg in Connachta: Mag Seired in Tethba; Mag Tochair in Tir Eogain; Mag Selmne in Araide; Mag Macha in Airgialla; Mag Muirthemne in Brega; Mag Bernsa in Laighne; Leccmag and Mag Moda in Mumu.

+ **43**. He won three battles agains the Fomoraig [or sea-rovers]: the battle of Badbgna in Connachta, of Cnamros in Laigne, of Murbolg in Dal Riada. After that, Nemed died of plague in Oilean Arda Nemid in Ui Liathain.

+ **44**. The progeny of Nemed were under great oppression after his time in Ireland, at the hands of More, son of Dela and of Conand son of Febar [from whom is the Tower of Conand named, which to-day is called Toirinis Cetne. In it was the great fleet of the Fomoraig]. Two thirds of the progeny, the wheat, and the milk of the people of Ireland (had to be brought) every Samain to Mag Cetne. Wrath and sadness seized on the men of Ireland for the burden of the tax. They all went to fight against the Fomoraig. They had three champions, Semul son of Iarbonel the Soothsayer son of Nemec, Erglan son of Beoan son of Starn son of Nemed, Fergus Red-Side son of Nemed. Thirty thousand on sea, other thirty thousand on land, these assaulted the tower. Conand and his progeny fell.

+ **45**. So, after that capture, More son of Dela came upon the, with the crews of three-score ships, and they fell in a mutual slaughter. The sea came up over the people of Ireland, and not one of them fled from another, so severe was the battling: none escaped but one ship, in which there were thirty warriors. They went forth, parting from Ireland, fleeing from the sickness and taxation: Bethach died in Ireland of plague; his ten wives survivied him for a space of twenty-three years. Ibath and his son Baath went into the north of the world. Matach and Erglan and Iartach, the three sons of Beoan, went to Dobar and Iardobar in the north of Alba.

+ **46**. Semeon went in the lands of the Greeks. His progeny increased there till they amounted to thousands. Slavery was imposed upon them by the Greeks; they had to carry clay upon rough mountains so that they became flowery plains. Thereafter they were weary of their servitude, and they went in flight, five thousand strong, and made them ships of their bags: [or, as the Quire of Druim Snechta says, they stole the pinnaces of the king of Greece for coming therein]. Thereafter they came again into Ireland, their land of origin: that was at the end of two hundred and thirty years after Nemed. These are their five chiefs, Gand, Genand, Rudraige, Sengand and Slaine.

+ **47**. As for Fergus Red-Side and his son, Britain Mael of whom are all the Britons in the world, they took Moin Conain and filled with their progeny the great island, Britannia Insula: till Hengist and Horsa, the two sons of Guictglis, King of the Old Saxons, came and conquered them: and they drove the Britons over the borders of the Island. These are the adventures of the progeny of Nemed after the taking of Conand's Tower: unde the Historian cecinit:

> *Great Ireland which the Gaedil regulate,*
> *I tell some of her concerns:*
> *Great chiefs spear-armed took her,*
> *of the proud race of Adam.*

> *From Adam the truly tuneful, the ruthless,*
> *to the Flood, a tumult that was prepared,*

none warmed her very powerful household
except Cessair of the fifty maidens.

Except Bith and Ladru--let us relate it--
Fintan, with darkness of the land, no man found it,
who revealed the stately superiority of Ireland,
before the time of the Flood.

After the Flood of secret going three hundred years,
whoso relates it,
he who was a bright crown for deeds of valour,
Partholon son of Sera, comes.

Notwithstanding every stately psalm-canon,
the people of Partholon the sinner--
dead was the whole tally of his household,
upon the Old Plain, in the course of a week.

Six fives of years without increase,
without a guard, it was dark obscurity,
Desert was every side to the proud sea;
Not a person took it save Nemed.

Nemed with wrath (?) of them all,
with store of feters and valour,
he possessed the land of the warring of hosts,
after the destruction of the other companies.

He used to effect victory without hazards,
Nemed, with pride and intelligence:
the son of Agnomain with haughtiness,
although his troop was weak, it was stately.

Starn, who fell at the hands of Mac Faebuir,
Iarbonel the Soothsayer, who was joyous,
Ainnind with fetters of leather,
were the three venemous chieftains of Nemed.

Nemed who paid them in the matter of securities,
it was a pestilence of fire over a death-doom;
in his time, with a great noise of rushing,
there was an outburst--four lakes.

34

Loch Munremair, a pleasant sea,
of broad-ridged, firm fury;
Loch Dairbrech over a hedge of a king (?)
Loch Cal and Loch Ainnind.

Vigorously there were dug by his host
two forts with strength and firmness,
Raith Cindeich in which he apportioned weapons,
Raith Cimbaeith in Semne.

Cleared by him, it was a road of pleasure,
twelve plains of good eye (-prospect),
Mag Cera in Connachta of mists,
Mag Moda and Mag Eba.

Strong Mag Tochair was cleansed,
Leemag of the great plain of Muma,
Mag Bernsa with a mystery of great graces,
Mag Cuile Tolad, Mag Lughad.

Mag Sered of drying-up of a river,
Mag Semne of lightness of colouring,
Mag Luirg of little darkness of side,
Mag Muirthemne, Mag Macha.

The routs--a work to recount them--
which he broke against the warriors of Fomoire of much sharpness,
the battle of huge Morbole of great sharpness the battle of Badgna,
and the battle of Cnamros.

In the territory of Liathan by Muma,
the dark lord of slaughter died of plague:
with the rude company of clean grass
in Oilean Arda Nemid.

They were not in security as regards oppression--
the progeny which Nemed fertilised--
at the hands of Conaing with hard body
and at the hands of More son of Dela.

Two-thirds of their shapely children,

35

it was not generous against military weakness--
a lasting tax through ages of the world--
two-thirds of corn and of milk.

To hard Mag Cetna of weapons,
Over Eas Ruaid of wonderful salmon,
it was prepared against help,
against feasting (?) for them, every Samain eve.

Semeon son of joyful Iardan,
Fergus pure and generous, an effort of pride,
Erglan son of warlike Beoan,
were the three freemen for their hosts.

The host of Ireland with her troop came--
it was steppings a power--
a warrior-band who had blood through the body,
westward to the capture of Conaing's tower.

Conaing's tower with store of plunder
of a union of the crimes of hundreds of rapine,
a fortress of assembly of the art
of the rage of the Fomoire of the sea.

The men of Ireland after its capture,
with the great valour of the courses before them,
of these, tidings of loss,
none escaped except thirty of the children of Nemed.

They were not at peace regarding their inheritance,
that host with great valour of despair;
of the thirty noble warriors,
every chieftain went his ways.

Into the land of Greeks, the remnant of the troop
went Semeon, it was a road of happiness:
with wisdom over the pre-eminent division
went Fergus into Moin Conain.

Britan Mael son of the prince
free the multitude of tracks over streams,
son of Lethderg from Leemag

from whom are the Britons of the world.

Bethach under steps of forms of fame
died in Ireland according to truthfulness:
his ten wives behind him,
thereafter, for a space of twenty-three years.

Hundreds sprang from Semeon,
the Greeks thought them a numerous legion:
they were not accepted by the warriors
but were enslaved by the Greeks.

This was the order of the chieftains,
Carrying round bags--it was not fraught
with fame [of] clay upon a rocky stony mountain
so that it was a plain rich in flowers and flocks.

They departed with no treacherous covenant
upon the wrathful very black sea,
out of the captivity of hard fosterage
with ships and with bags.

These were their names of pride,
of the kings, spirited, with agility,
Gann, Genann with choice men of good divisions,
Rudraige, Sengann, Slanga.

The seed of Semeon of a row of spear-divisions,
a deed of pure will of purity of action-deeds;
The Galioin, men of the very scanty orderings,
The Fir Boig and the Fir Domnann.

Two hundred years, whoso relates it,
after Nemed, lustrous his deeds of valour,
till the Fir Bolg took the tuneful land of Ireland,
from the sea-pool of ocean.

Their sending, their measuring-out, endures;
they divided into five, without religion--
without a falling for their slender-sided sept--
pleasant Ireland, from Uisnech.

Let us give adoration to most righteous Christ
Who hath subdued the strongest floods;
His is the world with its generation,
His is every territory, His is Ireland.

The capture of Conaing's tower with valour
against Conaing the great, son of Faebar:
the men of Ireland came to it,
three brilliant chieftains with them.

Erglan son of Beoan son of Starn,
Semeon son of bitter Iardan,
before exile went the warrior of the plains,
the son of Nemed, Fergus Lethderg.

Three score thousands in brilliant wise
over land and over water,
that is the tally who went from home,
the children of Nemed, to the capture.

Torinis, island of the tower,
the fortress of Conaing son of Faebar;
by Fegus himself, a fighting of valour,
Conaing son of Faebar fell.

More son of Dela came there,
it was for a help to Conaing:
Conaing fell previously,
More thought it grave tidings.

Three score ships over the sea was the tally
with which More son of Dela came;
there encountered them before they came to land,
the children of Nemed with powerful strength.

The men of all Ireland in the battle,
after the coming of the Fomoraig,
the sea-surge drowned them all,
except thrice ten men.

Erglan, Matach, Iartacht the noble,
the three sons of Beoan son of Starn,

38

white his girdle, Bethach, Britan after the battle,
Baath the glorious, and Ibath.

Bechach, Bethach, Bronal, Pal,
Goirthigorn, German, Glasa,
Ceran, Gobran, Gothiam pure,
Gam, Dam, Ding and Deal.

Semeon, Fortecht, bright Gosten,
Grimaig, Guillius with cleverness,
Taman, Turrue, and Glas,
Feb, and Feran curl-haired.

Three tens on the tuneful sailing
went afterwards from Ireland:
in three they made divisions
after the capture of Conaing's Tower in the west.

The third of Bethach the victoriuous,
tuneful fame, from Toirinis to Boinn:
it is he who died in Inis Fail,
two years after Britan.

The third of Semeon son of noble Erglan
to Belach Conglais with horror;
the third of Britan, saith Ua Flaind,
from that to Conaing's Tower.

The children of Israel on a journey
at that time, out of Egypt;
and the children of Gaedel Glas,
were a-voyaging to Scythia.

O Christ fair, with beauty of appearance,
O King, apportioner of the haven of Paradise,
Into Thy heaven, famous the place,
O King of the world, mayest thou choose me!

+ **48**. Now as for the Fir Bolg, they brought five chieftains with them, ut dixi supra, to wit, Gann, Genann, Rudraige, Sengann, Slanga: those were the fivce sons of Dela. Their fivce wives next, Anust, Liber, Cnucha, Fuat, Etar: [unde dicitur]

Fuat, wife of Slanga, you do not think it crooked,
Etar wife to Gann with valour,
Anust wife of Sengann of the spears,
Cnucha who was wife of pure Genann.

Liber wife of Rudraige of the Road,
a people sweet, that was not narrow:
Rudraige, master of wiles,
I suppose, Fuat was his wife.

+ **49**. The Fir Bolg separated into three. With Slanga son of Dela son of
Loth his third [landed] in Inber Slaine: his Fifth is from Inber Colptha to
Comar Tri nUisce; a thousand men his tally. The second third landed in
Inber Dubglaisi with Gann and Sengann: two thousand were their tally,
Gann from Comar Tri nUisce to Belach Conglais, Sengann from Belach
Conglais to Luimneach - that is, over the two Fifths of Mumu. Genann and
Rudraige with a third of the host, they landed in Inber Domnann: [whence
they are called Fir Domnann}. Genann it is who was king over the Fifth of
Medb and Ailell; Rudraige over the Fifth of Conchobor - other two
thousand were his tally. Those are the Fir Bolg, the Fir Domnann, and the
Gailioin. As to the Fir Domnann, the creek takes its name from them. The
Fir Bolg - they were named from their bags. The Gailioin, from the
multitude of their javelins were they named. They made one Taking and
one princedom, for they were five brethren, the five sons of Dela son of
Loth. And in one week they took Ireland, [though the days were different].
On Saturday, the kalends of August, Slanga landed in Inber Slaine. On
Tuesday Gann and Sengann landed. On Friday Genann and Rudraige
landed: and thus is it one Taking, though they were differently styled. The
Gaileoin, from Slanga were they named. From Gann and Sengann were the
Fir Bolg named. The Fir Domnann were named from deepening the earth:
they were Genann and Rudraige with their followers. For they are all called
Fir Bolg, and thirty-seven years was the length of their Lordship over
Ireland. The five sons of Dela were the five kings of the Fir Bolg, i.e.,
Gann, Genann, Rudraige, Sengann, Slaine.

+ **50**. [Now these men, the Fir Bolg, were the progeny of Dela.] Slanga was
the eldest, son of Dela son of Loth son of Oirthet, son of Tribuat son of
Gothorb son of Gosten son of Fortech son of Semeon son of Erglan son of
Beoan son of Starn son of Nemed son of Agnomain. No king took, who
was called "of Ireland," till the Fir Bolg came. Nine kings of them took
Ireland. Slanga, one year - it is he who died of the Fir Bolg in Ireland at the

first. Rudraige, two years, till he died in Brug Bratruad. Gann and Genann, four years, till they died of plague in Fremaind. Sengann, five years, till he fell at the hands of Rindail son of Genann son of Dela. Rindail, six years, till he fell at the hands of Fodbgenid son of Sengann son of Dela in Eba Coirpre. Fodbgen, four years, till he fell in Mag Muirthemne at the hands of Eochu son of Rindail son of Genann son of Dela. Eochu son of Erc, ten years. There was no wetting in his time, save only dew: there was no year

without harvest. Falsehoods were expelled from Ireland in his time. By him was executed the law of justice in Ireland for the first time. Eochu son of Erc fell at the hands of three sons of Nemed son of Badra: he is the first king of Ireland who received his death-wound in Ireland [Unde Colum Cille cecinit "Dean moresnis a mic,"etc.]

+ **51.** The Fir Bolg gave them [the Tuatha De Danann] battle upon Mag Tuired; they were a long time fighting that battle. At last it broke against the Fir Bolg, and the slaughter pressed northward, and a hundred thousand of them were slain westward to the strand of Eochaill. There was the king Eochu overtaken, and he fell at the hands of the three sons of Nemed. Yet the Tuatha De Danann suffered great loss in the battle, and they left the king on the field, with his arm cut from him; the leeches were seven years healing him. The Fir Bolg fell in that battle all but a few, and they went out of Ireland in flight from the Tuatha De Danann, into Ara, and Ile, and Rachra and other islands besides. [it was they who led the Fomoraig to the second battle of Mag Tuired]. And they were in [those islands] till the time

of the Provincials over Ireland, till the Cruithne drove them out. They came
to Cairbre Nia Fer, and he gave them lands; but they were unable to remain
with him for the heaviness of the impost which he put upon them.
Thereafter they came in flight before Cairbre under the protection of Meldb
and Ailill, and these gave them lands. This is the wandering of the sons of
Umor. [Oengus son of Umor was king over them in the east], and from
them are named those territories, Loch CIme from Cime Four-Heads son of
Umor, the Point of Taman in Medraige from Taman son of Umor, the Fort
of Oengus in Ara from Oengus, the Stone-heap of Conall in Aidne from
Conall, Mag Adair from Adar, Mag Asail from Asal in Mumu also. Menn
son of Umor was the poet. They were in fortresses and in islands of the sea
around Ireland in that wise, till Cu Chulaind overwhelmed them.

+ **52**. Those are the kings of the Fir Bolg and their deaths; unde poeta
cecinit

The Fir Bolg were here for a season
in the great island of the sons of Mil;
the five chiefs which they brought with them
from over yonder I know their names.

A year had Slanga, this is true,
till he died in his fine mound;
the first man of the Fir bolg of the peaks
who died in the island of Ireland.

Two years of Rudraige the Red,
till he died in Brug Brat-ruaid,
four of Genann and of Gann,
till plague slew them in Fremaind.

Five years of Sengann--they were reposeful--
till Fiachu son of Starn slew him;
five others--it was through battle--
Fiachu Cendfhindan was king.

Fiachu Cendfhindan before all,
his name endures forever;
white-headed all, without reproach,
were the kine of Ireland in his presence.

Till he fell at the hands of red Rindail,
he got six [years] with his free host;

The grandson of Dela fell then in Eba,
at the hands of Odbgen.

Four to noble Odbgen till the battle
of Murthemne of the nobles:
Odbgen died without reproach
at the hands of the son of Erc, of lofty Eochu.

Ten years to Eochu son of Erc,
he found not the border-line of weakness:
till they slew him on the battlefield,
the three sons of Nemed son of Badra.

Till Rinnal grew, there was no point at all
upon a weapon in Ireland;
upon harsh javelins there was no fair-covering,
but their being rushing-sticks.

In the time of Fodbgen thereafter
there came knots through trees:
the woods of Ireland down
till then were smooth and very straight.

The pleasant Tuatha De Danann
brought spears with them in their hands:
with them Eochu was slain,
by the seed of Nemed of strong judgement.

The names of the three excellent sons of Nemed
were Cessarb, Luam, and Luachra:
it is they who slew the first king with a point,
Eochu son of Erc, in Ireland.

Thereafter the Tuatha De fought for the Fir Bolg,
it was a rought appearance.
They took away their goods
and their lordship from the Men.

+ **53.** Fintan cecinit of the division of the Provinces –

The five parts of Ireland
between sea and land,

I entreat the fair candles
of every province among them.

From Drobais swift and fierce,
is the holy first division to
the Boyne white and vast
south from white Bairche.

From the Boyne, tuneful and whitely-glowing
with hundreds of harbours
To the Meeting with sound of assembled waves
of the cold Three Waters.

From that same
Meeting with nimble
From the Bel of the brave Cu
who is called 'glas.'

From Lumnech of huge ships--
broad its surface--
To Drobais of armed multitudes,
pure, on which a sea laugheth.

Knowledgeable prostration,
pathways are related,
perfection in the matter of correction
towards a road into five.

The points of those provinces
to Uisnech did they lead,
Each of them out of its ....
..... till it was five.

The progeny of Semeon were all the Gaileoin and Fir Domnann. Thirty years after Genann and Rudraige, the Tuatha De Danann came into Ireland.

+ **54.** Thereafter the progeny of Bethach son of Iarbonel the Soothsayer son of Nemed were in the northern islands of the world, learning druidry and knowledge and prophecy and magic, till they were expert in the arts of pagan cunning.

book iv

+ **55**. So that they were the Tuatha De Danann who came to Ireland. In this wise they came, in dark clouds. They landed on the mountains of Conmaicne Rein in Connachta; and they brought a darkness over the sun for three days and three nights.

+ **56**. They demanded battle of kingship of the Fir Bolg. A battle was fought between them, to wit the first battle of Mag Tuired, in which a hundred thousand of the Fir Bolg fell. Thereafter they [the TDD] took the kingship of Ireland. Those are the Tuatha Dea - gods were their men of arts, non-gods their husbandmen. They knew the incantations of druids, and charioteers, and trappers, and cupbearers.

+ **57**. It is the Tuatha De Danann who brought with them the Great Fal, [that is, the Stone of Knowledge], which was in Temair, whence Ireland bears the name of "The Plain of Fal." He under whom it should utter a cry was King of Ireland; until Cu Chulainn smote it, for it uttered no cry under him nor under his fosterling, Lugaid, son of the three Finds of Emain. And from that out the stone uttered no cry save under Conn of Temair. Then its heart flew out from it [from Temair] to Tailltin, so that is the Heart of Fal which is there. It was no chance which caused it, but Christ's being born, which is what broke the owers of the idols.

+ **58**. Now Nuadu Airgetlam was king over the Tuatha De Danann for seven years before their coming into Ireland, until his arm was hewn from him in the first battle of Mag Tuired. Eidleo son of Alldai, he was the first man of the Tuatha De Danann who fell in Ireland, by the hand of Nercon ua Semeoin, in the first battle of Mag Tuired. Ernmas, and Echtach, and Etargal, and Fiachra, and Tuirill Piccreo fell in the same battle. Bress son of Elada took the kingship of Ireland post, to the end of seven years, till the arm of Nuadu was healed: a silver arm with activity in every finger and every

joint which Dian Cecht put upon him, Credne helping him.

+ **59**. Tailltiu daughter of Mag Mor king of Spain, queen of the Fir Bolg, came after the slaughter was inflicted upon the Fir Bolg in that first battle of Mag Tuired to Coill Cuan: and the wood was cut down by her, so it was a plain under clover-flower before the end of a year. This is that Tailtiu who was wife of Eochu son of Erc king of Ireland till the Tuatha De Danann slew him, ut praediximus: it is he who took her from her father, from Spain; and it is she who slept with Eochu Garb son of Dui Dall of the Tuatha De Danann; and Cian son of Dian Cecht, whose other name was Scal Balb, gave her his son in fosterage, namely Lugh, whose mother was Eithne daughter of Balar. So Tailltiu died in Tailltiu, and her name clave thereto and her grave is from the Seat of Tailltiu north-eastward. Her games were performed every year and her song of lamentation, by Lugh. With gessa and feats of arms were they performed, a fortnight before Lugnasad and a fortnight after: under dicitur Lughnasadh, that is, the celebration or the festival of Lugh. Unde Oengus post multum tempus dicebat, "the nasad of Lug, or the nasad of Beoan [son] of Mellan."

+ **60**. To return to the Tuatha De Danann. Nuadu Airgatlam fell in the last battle of Mag Tuired, and Macha daughter of Ernmas, at the hands of Balar the strong-smiter. In that battle there fell Ogma son of Elada at the hands of Indech son of the De Dmnann, king of the Fomoire. Bruidne and Casmael fell at the hands of Ochtriallach son of Indech. After the death of Nuadu and of those men, Lug took the kingship of Ireland, and his grandfather Balar the Strong-smiter fell at his hands, with a stone from his sling. Lugh was forty years in the kingship of Ireland after the last battle of Mag Tuired, and there were twenty-seven years between the battles.

+ **61**. Then Eochu Ollathair, the great Dagda, son of Elada, was eighty years in the kingship of Ireland. His three sons were Oengus and Aed and Cermat Coem; the three sons of Dian Cecht, Cu and Cethen and Cian.

+ **62**. Dian Cecht had three sons, Cu, Cehten and Cian. Miach was the fourth son though many do not reckon him. His daughter was Etan the Poetess, and Airmed the she-leech was the other daughter: and Coirpre, son of Etan was the poet. Crichinbel and Bruidne and Casmael were the three satirists. Be Chuille and Dianan. were the two she-farmers. The three sons of Cermad son of The Dagda were Mac Cuill, Mac Cecht, Mac Griene: Sethor and Tethor and Cethor were their names. Fotla and Banba and Eriu were their three wives. Fea and Nemaind were the two wives of Net, a quo Ailech Neit. Flidais, of whom is the "Cattle of Flidais"; her four daughters were Argoen and Be Chuille and Dinand and Be Theite. The two royal oxen were Fea and Femen, of whom are the Plain of Fea and the Plain of Femen. Those were two faithful oxen. Torc Triath was king of the boars, from whom is Mag Treitherne. Cirba was king of the wethers, from whom is Mag Cirba. Math son of Umor was the druid. Badb and Macha and Anand, of whom are the Paps of Anu in Luachar were the three daughters of Ernmas the she-farmer. Goibniu the smith, Luicne the carpenter, Creidne the wright, Dian Cecht the leech.

+ **63**. Delbaeth after The Dagda, ten years in the kingship of Ireland, till he fell, with his son Ollom, at the hands of Caicher son of Nama, frater of Nechtan. Fiacha son of Delbaeth took the kingship of Ireland after his father, other ten years, till he fell, along with Ai son of Ollom, at the hands of Eogan Inbir. Twenty-nine years had the grandsons of The Dagda in the kingship of Ireland, to wit Mac Cuill, Mac Cecht, and Mac Greiene: they divided Ireland into three parts. To them came the Gaedil to Ireland, so that

47

they fell by the hands of three sons of Mil, avenging Ith, Cuailnge, and Fust, of the three sons of Breogan.

+ **64**. Nuadu Airgetlam son of Echtach son of Etarlam son of Ordam son of Aldui son of Tat son of Tavarn son of Enda son of Baath son of Ebath son of Bethach son of Iarbonel son of Nemed son of Agnomain son of Pamp son of Tat son of Sera son of Sru son of Esru son of Braimend son of Rathacht son of Magoth son of Iafeth son of Noe. Neit son of Indui son of Alldui son of Tat, Fiachna son of Delbaeth son of Ogma son of Elada son of Delbaeth son of Net, Ai son of Ollam son of Delbaeth son of Ogma son of Elada. Lug son of Cian son of Dian Cecht son of Esarg son of Net son of Indui son of Alldui, he is the first who brought chess-play and ball-play and horse-racing and assembling into Ireland, unde quidam cecinit. Lug son of Ethliu, a cliff without a wrinkle, with him there first came a lofty assembly: after the coming of Christ, it is no idle proclamation Conchobar the wise and violent died. Caicher and Nechtan, the two sons of Nama son of eochu Garb son of Dui Temen son of Bres son of Delbaeth son of Net. Siugmall son of Corpre Crom son of Eremair son of Delbaeth son of Ogma. Oengus mac Oc and Aed Caem and Cermait Milbel, those are the three sons of the Dagda. Corpre the poet son of Tuar son of Tuirell son of Cait Conaichend son of Orda son of Alldui son of Tat. Galia son of Oirbsen son of Elloth son of Elada son of Delbaeth son of Net. Orbsen was the name of Manannan at first, and from him is named Loch Orbsen in Connachta. When Manannan was being buried, it is then the lake burst over the land, [through the burial]. The six sons of Delbaeth son of Ogma son of Elada son of Delbaeth son of Net, were Fiachra, Ollam, Indui, Brian, Iucharba, Iuchar. Donann the daughter of the same Delbaeth was mother of the three last, Brian, Iucharba and Iuchar. These were the three gods of Danu, from whom is named the Mountain of the Three gods. And that Delbaeth had the name Tuirell Bicreo. Tuirill son of Cait moreover was the grandfather of Corpre the poet, and Etan d. Dian Cecht was mother of that Tuirill. The three sons of Cermait, moreover, ut diximus; Mac Cuill - Sethor, the hazel his god; Mac Cecht - Tethor, the ploughshare his god; Mac Greine - Cethor, the sun his god. Fotla was wife of Mac Cecht, Banba of Mac Cuill, Eriu of Mac Greine. Those were the three daughters of Fiachna son of Delbaeth. Ernmas daughter of Etarlam son of Nuada Airgetlam was mother of those three women, and mother of Fiachna and Ollom. Ernmas had other three daughters, Badb and Macha and Morrigu, whose name was Anand. Her three sons were Glon and Gaim and Coscar. Boind daughter of Delbaeth son of Elada. Fea and Neman, the two wives of Net son of Indiu, two daughters of Elemar of the Brug. Uillend son of Caicher son of Nuadu Airgetlam. Bodb of the Mound of Femen, son

of Eochu Gab son of Dui Temen son of Bres son of Elada son of Delbaeth
son of Net. Abean son of Bec-Felmas son of Cu son of Dian Cecht, the
poet of Lugh. En son of Bec-En son of Satharn son of Edleo son of Alda
son of Tat son of Taburn. At Tat son of Tabourn the choice of the Tuatha
De Danann unite. Of that the historian sang-

Ireland with pride, with weapons,
hosts spread over her ancient plain,
westward to the sunset were they plunderers,
her chieftains of destruction around Temair.

Thirty years after Genand
goblin hosts took the fertile land;
a blow to the vanquished People of Bags
was the visit of the Tuatha De Danann.

It is God who suffered them, though He restrained them--
they landed with horror, with lofty deed,
in their cloud of mighty combat of spectres,
upon a mountain of Conmaicne of Connacht.

Without distinction to descerning Ireland,
Without ships, a ruthless course
the truth was not known beneath the sky of stars,
whether they were of heaven or of earth.

If it were diabolic demons
the black-cloaked agitating expedition,
it was sound with ranks, with hosts:
if of men, it was the proteny of Bethach.

Of men belonging to law (is)
the greeborn who has the strong seed:
Bethach, a swift warrior-island (?)
son of Iarbonel son of Nemed.

They cast no assembly or justice
about the place of Fal to the sunset:
there was fire and fighting
at last in Mag Tuired.

The Tuatha De, it was the bed of a mighty one,

49

around the People of Bags fought for the kingship:
in their battle with abundance of pride,
troops of hundreds of thousands died.

The sons of Elada, glory of weapons,
a wolf of division against a man of plunder:
Bres from the Brug of Banba of wise utterance,
Dagda, Delbaeth, and Ogma.

Eriu, though it should reach a road-end,
Banba, Fotla, and Fea,
Neman of ingenious versicles,
Danann, mother of the gods.

Badb and Macha, greatness of wealth, Morrigu--
springs of craftiness,
sources of bitter fighting
were the three daughters of Ernmas.

Goibniu who was not impotent in smelting,
Luichtne, the free wright Creidne,
Dian Cecht, for going roads of great healing,
Mac ind Oc, Lug son of Ethliu.

Cridinbel, famous Bruinde,
Be Chuille, shapely Danand,
Casmael with bardism of perfecdtion,
Coirpre son of Etan, and Etan.

The grandsons of the Dagda, who had a triple division (?)
divided Banba of the bugle-horns; let us tell of the
princes of excellence of hospitality,
the three sons of Cermat of Cualu.

Though Ireland was multitudes of thousands
they divided her land into thirds:
great chieftains of deeds of pride,
Mac Cuill, Mac Cecht, Mac Greine.

He swept them clean from their land, did the Son of God,
from the royal plain which I make manifest:
for all the valour of their deeds,

of their clear division, their seed is not over Ireland.

It is Eochu without enchantment of leapings who fashions
the distinction of his good quatrains;
but knowledge of the warriors when he relates it,
though he enumerates them, he adores them not.

Adore ye the name of the King who measured you,
who apportions every truth which he (Eochu) narrates:
who hath released every storm which we expect,
who hath fashioned the pleasant land of Ireland.

Tanaide sang:

The Tuatha De Danann under obscurity,
a people without a covenant of religion;
whelps of the wood that has not withered,
people of the blood of Adam's flesh.

Nobles yonder of the strong people,
people of the withered summit, let us relate,
in the course in which we are,
their periods in their kingdom.

A space of seven years oq Nuadu noble--
stately over the fair-haired compnay,
the rule of the man large-breasted,
flaxen-maned before his coming into Ireland.

In Mag Tuired, heavy with doom,
where fell a champion of the battle,
from the white defender of the world--
his arm of princedom was lopped off

Seven years of Bres, which was not a white space,
through its fair prospect for the song-abbot,
in the princedom over the plain, generous in nuts,
till the arm of Nuadu was healed.

Nuadu after that twenty years,
he brought the fairy-folk a-hosting,
till Lugh the spear-slaughterous was made king--

51

the many-crafted who cooled not.

Forty to Lugh--it was balanced--
in the kingship over the Palace of Banba;
he reached no celestial bed of innocence;
eighty to The Dagda.

Ten years to vehement Delbaeth
till one wise in course and royal (?) arrived,
faultness over the brink of the ocean--
ten other to Fiachna.

Twenty-nine years, I have proclaimed it,
over every peace--land of Ireland,
in the kingdom over Banba eduringly great
had the grandons of The Dagda skilled in denseng.

Thereafter the sons of Mil came,
they arrived to redden them--
children of the great hero
who burst out of Spain without growing cold.

Till the deedful Gaedil wounded them,
without a troop, through their cunning,
it is not a matter of fable or of folly
that small was the weakness of the Tuatha.

Fland Mainstrech cecinit

Hearken, ye sages without sorrow,
if it be your will that I relate the deaths yonder,
with astuteness, of the choise of
the Tuatha De Danann.

Edleo son of Alldai yonder,
the first man of the Tuatha De
Danann who fell in virgin Ireland,
by the hand of Nerchon grandson of Semeon.

Ernams, high her valour, fell,
Fiachra, Echtach, Etargal,
Tuirill Picreo of Baile Breg

in the first batle of Mag Tuired.

Elloth with battle fell--
the father, great and rough, of
Manannan--and perfect, fair Donand,
at the hands of De Domnand of the Fomoraig.

Cethen of Cu died
of horror in Aircheltra;
Cian far from his home did Brian,
Iucharba dn Iuchar slay.

Of a stroke of the pure sun
died Cairpre the great, son of Etan:
Etan died over the pool of sorrow
for white-headed Cairpre.

In Mag Tuired, it was through battle
Nuadu Airgetlam fell: and Macha
--that was after Samhain--by the hand of Balar
the strong-smiter.

Ogma fell, without being weak
at the hands of Indech son of De Domnann:
breasted Casmael the good fell at the
hands of Oichtriallach son of Indech.

Now of painful plague died
Dian Cecht and Goibnenn the smith:
Liughne the wright fell along
with them by a strong fiery dart.

Creidne the pleasant artificer
was drowned on the lake-sea, the sinister pool,
fetching treasures of noble gold to
Ireland from Spain.

Bress died in Carn ui Neit by the treachery of Lug,
with no fullness of falsehood:
for him it was a cause of quarrel
indeed drinking bog-stuff in the guise of milk.

53

De Chuille and faithful Dianann,
both the farmeresses died,
an evening with druidry,
at the last, by gray demons of air.

He fell on the strand eastward in the trenches of Rath
Ailig, Did Indui the great,
son of pleasant Delbaith, at the
hands of Gann, a youth bold, white-fisted.

Fea, lasting was his fame,
died at the end of a month after
his slaying at the same stronghold--we think it fitting--
for sorrow for Indui the white-haired.

Boind died at the combat
at the wellspring of the son of noble Nechtan:
Aine daughter of the Dagda died for the
love that she gave to Banba.

Cairpre fell--remember thou!
by the hand of Nechtan son of Nama:
Nechtan fell by the poison at the hands of
Sigmall, grandson of Free Midir.

Abean son of cold Bic-felmais,
the bard of Lug with full victory,
he fell by the hand of Oengus
without reproach in front of Midir of mighty deeds.

Midir son if Indui yonder
fell by the hand of Elemar:
fell Elemar, fit for fight,
at the hands of Oengus the perfect.

Brian, Iucharba, and Iuchar there,
the three gods of the Tuatha De Danann
were slain at Mana over the bright sea
by the hand of Lug son of Ethliu.

Cermait son of the divine Dagda Lug
... (?)

wounded him it was a sorrow of grief
upon the plain in the reign of Eochu Ollathair.

Cermat Milbel the mighty fell
at the hands of harsh Lug son of Ethliu,
in jealousy about his wife, great the fashion,
concerning whom the druid lied unto him.

By the hand of Mac Cecht
without affection the harper fell:
moreover Lug fell over the wave,
by the hand of Mac Cuill son of Cermat.

Aed son of The Dagda fell at the hands
of Corrchend the fair, of equal valour;
without deceit, it was a desire of
strictness, after he had gone to his wife iniquitously.

Corrcend from Cruach fell
--the harsh very swift champion,
by the stone which he raised on the strand
over the grave of shamefaced Aed.

Cridinbel squiting and crooked fell
--the chief spell-weaver of the Tuatha De Danann--
of the gold which he found in the idle Bann,
by the hand of The Dagda, grandson of Delbaeth.

As he came from cold Alba he,
the son of The Dagda of
ruddy form, at the outlet of Boinn,
over here, there was Oengus drowned.

The only son of Manannan from the bay,
the first love of the aged woman,
the tender youth fell in the plain at the
hands of Idle Bennan, on the plain of Breg.

Net son of Indui and his two wives,
Badb and Neman without deceit,
were slain in Ailech without blame by
Nemtuir the Red, of the Fomoraig.

55

Fuamnach the white (?) who was wife of Midir,
Sigmall and Bri without faults,
In Bri Leith, it was full vigour, they
were burnt by Manannan.

The son of Allot fell, with valour,
the rich treasure, Manannan,
in the battle in harsh Cuillend by the hand of
Uillend of the red eyebrows.

Uillend with pride fell
at the hands of Mac Greine with pure victory:
the wife of the brown Dagda
perished of plague of the slope in Liathdruim.

The Dagda died of a dart of gore in the Brug
--it is no falsehood--
wherewith the woman Cethlenn gave him mortal hurt,
in the great battle of Mag Tuired.

Delbaeth and his son fell
at the hands of Caicher, the noble son of Nama:
Caicher fell at the idle Boinn,
at the hands of Fiachna son of Delbaeth.

Fiacha and noble Ai fell
before sound Eogan of the Creek:
Eogan of the cold creek fell
before Eochaid the knowing, hard as iron.

Eochaid of knowledge fell thereafter
At the hands of Ed and of Labraid:
Labraid, Oengus, Aed, fell
At the hands of Cermat of form all fair.

Eriu and Fotla with pride,
Mac Greine and Banba with victory,
Mac Cuill, Mac Cecht with purity in the battle of
Temair of clear wave.

Mac Cecht at the hands of noble Eremon:

Mac Cuill, of perfect Eber:
Eriu yonder, at the hands of Suirge
thereafter: Mac Greine of Amorgen.

Fotla at the hands of Etan with pride,
Of Caicher, Banba with victory,
Whatever the place wherein they sleep,
Those are the deaths of the warriors; hear ye.

Those are the adventures of the Tuatha De Danann.

book v

+ **65**. The taking of the Gaedil and their synchronizing, here below. As for the Gaedil, we have given their ventures from Iafeth son of Noe onward, and from the Tower of Nemrod, till we have left them at Breogan's Tower in Spain; and how they came from Egypt, and out of Scythia to the Maeotic Marshes, and along the Tyrrhene Sea to Crete and to Sicily; and we have further related how they took Spain by force. We shall now tell you below simply, how they came to Ireland.

+ **66**. Íth son of Breogan, [it is he] who saw Ireland at the first, on a winter's evening, from the top of Breogan's Tower; for thus is a man's vision best, on a clear winter's evening. Íth, with thrice thirty warriors, came to Ireland, and they landed on the "Fetid Shore" of the Headland of Corcu Duibne, what time they arrived. If we follow the Munster authorities, this is their route. they came thereafter into Corcu Duibne, into Ciarraige Luachra, into Luachair Dedad, into tim plain of Cliu, into Eile, into Tir Cell, along Mide, into the Territory of Luigne, over Sliab Guaire, past the woods of Fernmag, into Fossad Cláir of Fernmag, over the head of Shah Betheeh, into Shah Toad, into the swamp of Tir Sirláim, into the Territory of Modorn, into Mag Ítha, across the head of Loch Febail, into the Land of Net, to Ailech of Net. But, according to the Northerners, he sailed, as we have said, to Ireland, and landed on the "Fetid Shore" of Mag Iftha, on the Northern side of Ireland.

+ **67**. People came to hold converse with him on that strand, and each of them told their tidings mutually, through the Scotic language; fitting was that, seeing that on both sides they were of the progeny of Rifath Scot. they asked of them what was the name of this island. Inis Elga, said they; Mac Cuill, Mac Cécht, and Mac Gréine are its three kings. Who is its king? said Íth. They answered; (a) Mae Cuill, Mac Cécht, and Mac Gréine are the names of the three kings that are over it. [Now others say that it was shepherds who first met him, and gave him tidings.] Íth asked, Where those kings were! They said that Cathair Crofind - was the place where they were. Howbeit, that is not where they were--at the moment, but—-

+ **68**. There was in fact a convention of the men of Ireland at Ailech of Net, after the slaying of Net son of Innui of Ailech by the Fomoire. The three kings were dividing the cattle and the treasures of the king of Aileeh at the time. Íth son of Breogan came from Corco Duibne, into Ciarraige, and into

Luacliair Dedad, into the lowland of Clíu, thence Northward into the Éiles, into the land of Fir Cell, along Mide, into the territory of Luigne, over Sliabh Guaire, over the woods of Fernmag, into Fossad Cláir: of Fernmag, over the head of Sliabh Bethech, into Sliabh Tóád, into the Swamp of Tír Sírláim, into the territory of Modorn, into Mag nítha, to Ailech Néit. The three kings, Mac Cuill, Mac Cécht, Mac Gréine, were there, and they welcomed him (i.e. Íth son of Breogan), and told him the matter that was occupying them.

+ **69.** Íth surpassed the judges of Ireland in cunning and in argument; and lie settled every matter and every dispute that was before them. Then said Íth: Work just righteousness, for good is the land wherein ye dwell; plenteous its fruit, its honey, its wheat and its fish; moderate its heat and its cold. Within it is all that bade them farewell, and ye need. Thereafter he made for his ship, bade them farewell, and made for his ship.

+ **70.** [The first night afterwards [when] Íth went into Ireland after their arrival at Loch Sailech], demons slew one of his followers. He is the first who was slain in Ireland there, of the progeny of the Sons of Míl. Every harbour whereto tth would come in Ireland, after coasting every territory where it was, Mag Ítha is its name; Mag ftha at Lock Febail, the Lands of Íth at Locli Sailech, Mag Ítha among the Déssi, Mag Ítha at Luimnech.

+ **71.** It is then that a plot was laid by them to kill Íth, and they bade him begone out of Ireland; and he came away from them, from Ailech Mag Ítha. There was a pursuit after him as far as that, and he fell at their hands in Mag Ítha; unde Mag Ítha nominatur. So it was to avenge Íth that the sons of Míl [to wit, the Gáecil] came--for his [Íth's] body was carried to Spain.

+ **72.** Now, this is what learned men relate; that thirty-six leaders and nobles strong the Gáedil came. [Each of them had a ship, which makes thirty(-six) ships.] And four-and-twenty sertors had they, each of whom had a ship; and four-and-twenty servitors along with every servitor in every ship, again. These are the six and thirty chieftains who came into Ireland as Fintan son of Bochra recorded (who was born seven years before the Flood; till seven years of the reign of Diarmait mac Cerbaill, that was his [Fintan's] life) under the nurture of Finnian of Mag Bile, and of Colum Cille, and as Túan mac Cairll recorded in the presence of the Irish, and cf Finnian of Mag Bile, and as their pupils related, to wit Ladcend son of Bairche, and Colmán son of Comgellán, and Cenn Fáelad son of Ailill, and Senchan a. Colmán, Cú Alad from the Cruachans, and Bran of Boirenn, etc. Those are the pupils of Finnian and of Túán. And what they said was, that these are the thirty-six chieftains who entered Ireland as the Gaedil, namely the ten sons of Bregon (Íth being one of them)—Brego, Bile, Blad, Cualu, Cuailnge, Fúat, Muirthemne, Eibleo, Íth, Nár: the single son of Bile, Míl of Spain (Galam was his proper name): the seven sons of Míl, Donn, Colptha, Amorgen, Éber, Ír, Érimón, Érech Febria and Érennán, the youngest of the family. The three sons of Érimón; Muimne, Luigne, Laigne; also Palap and Írial Fáid (but in Ireland itself was Írial born) the son of Érimón. And he is called Nuadu Airgetlám. Nuadu Airgetlám had two sons, Glas a quo Síl nArgetrois, and Fir Nuadat; and they took the princedom over Ireland; for Nuadu was not in partnership with them, for he was a youth, and there was no disturbance of division among them, on account of his piety to his brethren; but he used to feed and clothe every child born to him, and he suppressed the children of the one and enlarged those of the other for their piety; for what learned men say is, that every princely family that is in Ireland, save the Eoganacht, is of the seed of Nuadu Airgetlám. Another family is reckoned as having been born to Érimón in Ireland, namely Alan, Eidenn, Aine, Caithiar, Caitheair, Cerna. The four sons of Éber Finn, Ér, Orba, Ferón, Fergna. And learned men reckon that lie had children in Ireland, to wit Conmáel son of Éber, who took the kingship of Ireland and of Alba, and Caur, Corand, Edar, Airb, Airbe. The ten champions further, Caicher, Fulmán, Mantán, Sétga, Suirge, Sobairche, Én son of Oice, Ún son of Uice, Étán, Goisten. Or they were three son of Nár son of Breogan, and Gosten was the brother of Setga. Those are the names of the ten champions; Bres, Búas, Buaigne, the three sons of Tigernbard son of Brigi son of Breogan. Or perhaps Brigi son of Brig had a son Bile. And there came also Lugaid son of Ith, the hard valorous powerful warrior, to avenge his father. So that those are the company of chieftains who came into Ireland with the Sons of Míl, the ten sons of Breogan, and the eight sons of Míl, the five sons of Érimón, and the four sons of Éber Finn, and the ten champions. And there came thither Gosten and Sétga and Íth son of Breogan. And learned men say that Míl came not into Ireland; and others say that the three kings died of plague before coming into Ireland, namely Míl son of Bile, and Oige. and Uige, the two sons of Allod son of Noenel. The twenty-four servitors as under; Aidne, Al, Assal, Mede, Morba, Mide, Cuib, Clíu, Cera, Saer, Slán, Life, Line, Ligen, Traig, Dul, Adal, Aire, Dése, Dela, Fea, Femen, Fera. Moreover Lugaid son of Íth came also, the hard valorous warrior with the strength of an hundred, to avenge his father along with them all. Those are the names of the chief servitors, these are the names of the subordinate sbrvitors below, who are not very prominent in the books: Medar, Ladar, Medon, Pida, Cath, Ruis, Cailna, Mad, Dena, Caeha, Bonn, Finnu, Cer,

Coirche, Meadba, Ailim, Bir, Baschon, Forena, Lugba, Sega, Seilgenn, Seg, Mar, Aig. They say that Éber had sons besides these, Caur, Capa, Corunn, Edor, Arb, Airrbe. Éremón had other six sons, Edenn, A[l]an, Ailie, Caichear, and Caieher Cernda; and that family is not usually brought into prominence.

+ **73.** One of the eight Sons of Míl, Érannán, the youngest of the family, he it was who went up the mast to spy out Ireland, and fell from the mast into the sea [on to the rock, F.]. And his grave is in Inber Scéne, and the grave of Scéne wife of Amorgen on the other side. She died on the sea at their estuary, and Amorgen said: The harbour wherein we shall land, shall bear the name of Scéne. The sons of Míl made a contention in rowing as they came to Ireland from the place where they saw Ireland away from them; and Ír son of Míl advanced the length of a murchrech [possibly the mythical "nine waves" --MJ] beyond every ship. Éber Donn, the eldest of the family, was envious, and he said—

> *It is not lucky*
> *that Ír leapeth beyond Íth,*

—[that is, beyond Lugaid son of Íth]. Then the oar that was in the hand of Ír broke, so that he fell backward, and died in the following night; and his body was taken to Sceilic, behind the Southern promontory of Corcc Duibne. Every time that the Sons of Míl came up with Ireland, the demons would frame that the port was, as it were, a hog's back; whence Ireland is called "Hog island". They skirted around Ireland three times, and landed at last in Inber Scéne. Sorrowful were Éber Finn and Érimón and Amorgen after the death of their brother; and they said: It were right that Éber Donn should have no share of the land, regarding which he was envious of his brother Ir. On the morrow Scéne and Érannán were buried in Inber Scéne. They two were both buried; their mounds and their graves are still there, side by side. Then said Amorgen—

> *Though it be the grave of Scene—so it was [hitherto]—*
> *(but the name of Scene shall remain upon it)*
> *it shall be the grave of Erannán, till he come,*
> *from God came the death of this poet.*

+ **74.** As he set his right foot upon Ireland, Amorgen Glúingel son of Míl spoke this poem—
> *I am Wind on Sea,*
> *I am Ocean-wave,*

61

I am Roar of Sea,
I am Bull of Seven Fights,
I am Vulture on Cliff,
I am Dewdrop,
I am Fairest of Flowers,
I am Boar for Boldness,
I am Salmon in Pool,
I am Lake on Plain,
I am a Mountain in a Man,
I am a Word of Skill,
I am the Point of a Weapon (that poureth forth combat),
I am God who fashioneth Fire for a Head.
Who smootheth the ruggedness of a mountain?
Who is He who announceth the ages of the Moon?
And who, the place where falleth the sunset?
Who calleth the cattle from the House of Tethys?
On whom do the cattle of Tethys smile?
Who is the troop, who the god who fashioneth edges
in a fortress of gangrene?
Enchantments about a spear? Enchantments of Wind?

Item Amorgen cecinit—-
A fishful sea!
A fruitful land!
An outburst of fish
Fish under wave,
In streams (as) of
A rough sea!
birds,
A white hail
With hundreds of salmon,
Of broad whales!
A harbour-song—
An outburst of fish,
A fishful sea!

At the end of three days and three nights thereafter the Sons of Míl broke the battle of Sliab Mis against demons and Fomoraig, that is, against the Túatha Dé Danann. It is there that Fás (sic lege) fell, the wife of Ún son of Uicce, after whom "the grave of Fás" is named, between Sliab Mis and the sea. Scota d. Pharao king of Egypt, also died in that battle—the wife of Érimón son of Míl. For Míl son of Bile went a-voyaging into Egypt, four ships' companies strong, and he took Scota to wife, and Érimón took her after him. In that night on which the sons of Míl came into Ireland, was the burst of Loch Luigdech in Iar-Mumu. "Shah Mis"—that means the worst mountain which they found after coming into Ireland, for there they fought their first battle in Ireland.

+ **75**. Lugaid son of Íth was bathing in Loch Luigdech; Fial, wife of Lugaid, bathed in the river that flows out of the lake. Her husband went to her naked, and she saw the nakedness of her husband, and died for shame. Unde Loch Luigdech, and Fial, and Inber Féile nominantur.

+ **76**. The Sons of Míl fought the battle of Life; there were monsters in shapes of giants which the Túatha Dé Danann had summoned to themselves by druidry. The Sons of Míl (Éber, Érimón and Ír), fought the battle valiantly. The horse (gabar) of Érimón fell there, unde Gabar Life rwminatur. They came thereafter till they were in the mountain over against [Loch] Dergderc.

+ **77**. The sons of Míl had colloquy with Banba in Sliab Mis. Said Banba unto them: If it be to take Ireland ye have come, not right were the good-fortune in which ye have come. It is by necessity, said Amorgen Glúingel, the poet. A gift from you to me then, said she. What gift? said they. That my name may be on this island, said she. What is thy name? said they. Banba, said she. Let it be a name for this island, said Amorgen. The Book of Druim Snechta says that Amorgen enquired after her race. Of the progeny of Adam am I, said she. Which race of the sons of Noe is thine! said he. I am older than Noe, said she; on a peak of a mountain was I in the Flood; to this present mound the waves of the Flood attained. Therefore, is it called Tul Tuinne? [But the foregoing is a surprising extract.] Thereafter they sing spells against her, and drive her away from them.

+ **78**. They had colloquy with Fotla in Eblinne. She spake with them in like manner, and desired that her name should be upon the island. Said Amorgen: Let Fotla be a name upon this island.

+ **79**. They had colloquy with Ériu in Uisnech. She said unto them:
Warriors, said she, welcome to you. Long have soothsayers had
[knowledge of] your coming. Yours shall be this island for ever; and to the
east of the world there shall not be a better island. No race shall there be,
more numerous than yours. Good is that, said Amorgen; good is the
prophecy. Not right were it to thank her, said Éber Donn, eldest of the sons
of Míl; thank our gods and our own might. To thee 'tis equal, said Ériu;
thou shalt have no profit of this island, nor shall thy progeny. A gift to me,
ye sons of Míl, and ye children of Breogan, said she; that my name shall be
on this island. It shall be its principal name, said Amorgen. The Book of
Druim Snechta says that it was in Sliab Mis that Ériu had colloquy with
them, and that she formed great hosts to oppose them, so that they were
fighting with them. But their druids and poets sang spells to them, and they
saw that these were only sods of the mountain peat-mosses. (Thence comes
the name Sliab Misse.) And that it was Fotla who had colloquy with them
in Uisnech.

+ **80**. The sons of Míl and of Bregon went on, till they were in Druim
Chain, that is, Temair. The three kings of Ireland, Mac Cuill, Mac Cécht,
and Mac Gréine, were there. They pronounced judgement against the Sons
of Míl, that they [themselves] should have the island to the end of three
days, free from assault, from assembly of battle, or from giving of
hostages; for they were assured that they (the invaders) would not return,
because druids would make spells behind them, so that they should not be
able to come again. We shall adjudge it, said Mac Cuill son of Cermat, as
Amorgen your own judge shall pronounce to you; for if he should give a
false judgement, he [aliter, you] would die at our hands. Give the
judgement, Amorgen, said Eber Donn. I pronounce it; said Amorgen. Let
this island be left to them. How far shall we go said Éber.. Past just nine
waves, said Amorgen. This is the first judgement given in Ireland.
Amorgen cecinit—-

Men, seeking a possession!
Over nine great green-shouldered waves,
Ye shall not go, unless with powerful gods!
Be it settled swiftly! Be battle permitted!

I adjust the possession
Of the land to which ye have come;
If ye like it, adjudge the right,
If ye like it not, adjudge it not—
I say it not to you, except with your good will.

+ **81**. They came southward from Temair as far as Inber Féile and Inber
Scéne, for it is there that their ships were. Then went they out, past nine
waves. The druids of Ireland and the poets sang spells behind them, so that
they were carried far from Ireland, and were in distress by reason of the
sea. A wind of wizards is this! said Éber Donn; look ye whether it—the
wind—-be over the mast. And it was not. Patience! said Airech, steersman
of the ship of Donn, till Amorgen come (Airech was the fosterling of
Amorgen). They all went forward, till they were in one place. Said Donn,
the eldest, This is a disgrace for our men of cunning, said he. 'Tis no
disgrace! said Amorgen; and he spake—-

I seek the land of Ireland,
Coursed be the fruitful sea,
Fruitful the ranked highland,
Ranked the showery wood,

Showery the river of cataracts,
Of cataracts the lake of poois,
Of pools the hill of a well,
Of a well of a people of assemblies,
Of assemblies of the king of Temair;
Temair, hill of peoples,
Peoples of the Sons of Mll,
Of Mil of ships, of barks;
The high ship Eriu,
Eriu lofty, very green,
An incantation very cunning,
The great cunning of the wives of Bres,
Of Bres, of the wives of Buaigne,
The mighty lady Eriu,
Erimón harried her,

—and a calming of the wind came to them forthwith.

+ **82**. Said Donn: I shall now, said he, put under the edge of spear and sword all that are in Ireland. And the wind rose against the ship wherein were Donn and Airech, two sons of Mil, and the ship wherein were Bres, Búas, and Buaighne; so that they were drowned at the Sandhills at Tech Duinn. The grave-mound of each man is there. And there, as some say, Díl, wife of Donn, was drowned. She was a daughter of Míl, and Érimón himself laid a sod upon her. This is a sod over Díl, said he. Unde Fotla nominatur, ut quidam putant.

+ **83**. Howbeit, Odba d. Míl, mother of the three sons of Érimón, of Muimne, Luigne, and Laigne, she it is whom Érimón deserted in Spain, taking Tea in her stead. But Odba came from the South in a ship, along with her sons, and they maintained her till she died in Odba. Unde Odba [dicitur]. As for Tea d. Lugaid son of Íth, she it was whom Érimón took instead of Odba; and she was to choose a mound in Ireland as her bridal portion. This is the marriage-price which she chose, Druim Chain, the mound which is Temair; Temair is Tea Mur, "the Wall of Tea (d. Lugaid son of Íth)." Lugaid means Lug Íth, that is, "Lug, who was less than his father."

+ **84**. Éremón with thirty ships sailed right-hand-wise against Ireland to the North-east. These are his chieftains: Brego, Muirthenme, Fáat, Cuailnge, Érimón, Éber son of Ír, Amorgen, Colptha, Muimne, Luigne, Laigne, Gosten, Sétga, Suirge, Sobairche. Further, these are the fourteen servitors:

Ai, Mdne, Assal, Mide, Cuib, Cera, Sér, Slán, Ligen, Dul, Adal, Traig, Line. Of them the historian sang—

> *Meadon, Meadair, Caeh, Dala,*
> *Lotan, Pita, Cath, Cuanna,*
> *Rus, Calna, Mag, is Deana,*
> *Cacha, Bonn, Findu, Buada.*

They landed in Inber Colptha; that is, Colptha son of Míl, he it is who landed at first, so that it is his name which is on the harbour; unde Inber Colptha.

+ **85.** As for the Sons of Breogan, they left no descendants, only their names upon the noble fortresses of Ireland.

+ **86.** There is no progeny reported of the warriors, Sétga, Gosten, Sobairche, and Suirge. Of Amorgen is Corcu Achrach in Éile, and the Orbraige, and Corcu Airtbinn, and Corcu Airtbi.

+ **87.** Éber son of Ír, of him are the progeny of Ollom Fotla and of Rudraige; all the Ulaid are of his progeny. Of his progeny are Conmaicne, Ciarraige, Corcomruad, and Corcu Duibne; Dál Moga Ruith (i.e Fir Maige Féne) and Laigse of Laigin, Arad Chliach and the seven Sogains.

+ **88.** As for Érimón, the leader of the expedition, of him is Leth Cuinn, i.e. the four families of Temair—-Conall, Colmán, Eogan, and Aed Sláine. Of him are the three Connachta, and Airgialla, Laigin, and Osraige, the Déssi of Mumu, and the Ernai of Mumu, of whom were the progeny of Deda, as well as Conaire the Great with his children (the men of Alba and of Dál Riata); and the Muscraige, and Corco Baiscinn. And of the Ernai of Mumu are Dál Fiatach, the kings of Ulaid; those are the progeny of Érimón. Of them also are the Fotharta, of whom came Brigit, and Fintan of Cluain Eidnech, Ui Ailella, and IJi Cheocháin. Of the Fotharta are all those. [Those are all the progeny of Érimón].

+ **89.** Éber remained in the South [with] thirty ships. These are his leaders—Bile, Míl, Cualu, Blád, Ebliu, Nár, Éber Donn, Éber Finn, Airech, Érannán, Lugaid, Ér, Orba, Ferón, Fergna, Én, Un, Etán, Caicher, Mantán, Fulmán. These are the servitors, of whom each man had a ship; Adar, Aire, Déisse, Dela, Clíu, Mórba, Fea, Life, Femen, Fera.

+ **90.** Bile and Míl, of their progeny are all the Gáedil. Cualu and Blad and

Ebliu left no progeny, only their names upon important mountains. Nár son of Bile, a quo Ros Náir. No progeny of the warriors is recorded, that is, of Ér, Étán, Caicher, Fulmán, Mantán. Éber Donn and Airech left no children, for they were drowned, as we have said. The four sons of Éber, Ér, Orba, Ferón, Fergna, had no children. They had a half-year in the kingship of Ireland, till Íriel slew them.

+ **91**. Lugaid son of Íth, five peoples came of him, to wit the family of Dáire Doimthech, namely the five Lugaids—Lugaid Cal, a quo the Calraige of Connachta, Lugaid Corr a quo the Corpraige, Lugaid Corp a quo Dál Coirpre of Cliu ut alii dicunt, Lugaid Oircthe a quo Corcu Oircthi, Lugaid Láeg, a quo Corcu Láegde; of whom was the son of Dairine, Lugaid mac Con. Ailill Ólom it is he who nurtured him; and he could not sleep with any save with Elóir, a hound which Aiiill possessed.

+ **92**. As for Éber Finn, of his progeny are Dál Cais, and Dál Cein, and Delbna, and the Northern Déssi, and Dál Moscorb, ut quidam putant; Dál Mathra, hUi Derduib, Cathraige, Éile, and Túath Tuirbi; and the Eoganacht of Caissel, of Áme, of Loch Loin, of Ráithlinn, of Glenn Amain, of Ara, and of Ros Airgit. Those are all the seed of Éber.

+ **93**. There was a contention between the sons of Míl concerning the kingship, that is, between Éber and Érimón. Amorgen was brought to them to arbitrate between them, and he said: The heritage of the chief, Donn, to the second, Érimón; and his heritage to Éber after him. But Éher would not accept that--only a division of Ireland. These are the first three judgements that were given among the sons of Míl in Ireland: the judgement that Amorgen gave in Temair, and that decision in Sliab Mis, and the decision that Amorgen gave in Cenn tSáile in Mumu upon the deer and roes and quadrupeds; as the poet said—

> *There did Amorgen give the judgement*
> *his neighbours conceal it not;*
> *after the battle of Mala, a fame without decay,*
> *between the hosts of the Sons of Mil.*

> *To each of them he apportioned his right,*
> *as they were a-hunting;*
> *each one received his lawful due at his hands,*
> *by the judgement of Amorgen, high and great.*

> *The first wounding of stags, it is known,*

be it a man or a hound that tears the skin,
to the stag-hounds, customary without fail,
there comes what is cast to them. (?)

The share of the skinner, so he [Amorgen] apportioned it,
a gulp (?) of the short brief neck;
to the coursing-dog the legs of the stag,
his should be a part that is not increased

The inward parts to the man who comes last,
whether he thinks the course good or bad,
it is certain that he is not entitled,
from it, to shares in the co-division.

A general division to everyone
thereafter—it is no vain course—
without commanding hither or thither
this is the judgement that Amorgen gave.

+ **94**. In the end there were six chieftains southward and seven chieftains northward who came there; and Éber had the kingship southward and Erimón the kingship northward. The six in the South were Éber himself, Lugaid son of Íth, Étán son of Oicce, Ún son of Uicce, Caicher, Fulman. The seven in the North were Érimón, Éber son of Ír, Amorgen, Gosten, Sétga, Sobairce, and the seventh rwas Surge. Of these matters did Roigne the poet speak, the son of Ugoine the Great, to Mál son of Ugoine his brother, when Mál asked him: Sing of thine expedition. Then is it that Raigne said—

Noble son of Ugoine,
How attains one to full knowledge of Ireland?
He arose from Scythia,
Did Feinius Farsaid himself;
Nél reached Egypt,
Remained awhile faithfully
With Pharao in journeys.
A betrothal of Nél, of Scota,
The conception of our father Gaedil,
The surname of "Scot" spread abroad
Did the fair daughter of Pharao.
The people of the Good God arrived together
With smiting of a great host.

Cincris was extinguished,
Drowned in the Red Sea.
They voyaged the sea-surface
Arrived at Scythia,
Which Eber Scot harried;
They smote Refioir,
Did Agnomain, Lamfind.
They sailed over Caspian
Entered on Liuis,
Made for Toirrian,
Followed on past Africa,
Arrived at Spain,
Where were conceived Erimon,
And Eber to Mile.
Soon Brego, Bile,
For avenging of Ith,
Grouped in their barks,
Sixty their number.
The men as they returned
Divided Ireland
Among twice six chieftains.
Let the truth of the history suffice!
I answer the question keenly.

+ **95**. Or they say that they were twice six men, namely the six sons of Míl and the six sons of Breogan—Érimón, Éber, Lugaid, Amorgen, Colptha, Ír; Brego, Bile, Fúat, Blad, Cualu, Cuailnge. In this wise did the Gáedil take Ireland; finit of the Takings of Ireland down to this.

www.ingramcontent.com/pod-product-compliance
Lightning Source LLC
Chambersburg PA
CBHW070938120626
46546CB00004B/1462